"*Imagine* gives you the tools to create from your core—not your conditioning. A must-read for modern leaders who value impact, alignment, and who want to live and build with intention."

——BABBA C. RIVERA, founder of Ceremonia, thought-leader

"The ultimate must-read manifestation book for anyone wanting to shift and supercharge their mindset. A transformational page-turner."

——EMMA MILDON, bestselling author of *The Soul Searcher's Handbook* and *Evolution of Goddess*

"In this beautiful book, Deganit and Tim lay out a clear and empowering path for our expansion—one rooted in compassion, justice, and healing for all. I can't think of two more generous guides nor a more uplifting path to our dreams."

——AMINA ALTAI, executive coach, speaker, and bestselling author of *The Ambition Trap*

"As a systems therapist and hypnotherapist who specializes in working with sensory-sensitive and queer folks, I love how *Imagine* provides a very practical, structured way to develop self-directive, self-empowering visualization and attention tools. Learning to take up space starts with taking up space in one's body. I recommend *Imagine* to my clients as a friendly guide to work with the profound and subtle power of their imagination."

——ANE AXFORD, LMFT, CHt, creator of *The Elements of Sensitivity Card Deck* and *subtleself.org*

"Deganit and Tim are masterful guides. They walk with integrity, intention, and so much heart. What I love about *Imagine* is how it unapologetically empowers the reader. It doesn't preach—it activates. It's a gift to every soul on a mission."

——JO-NÁ A. WILLIAMS, Esq, founder of J.A. Williams Law and Secure Your Empire

"*Imagine* is an inviting and practical guide to personal transformation. With clarity and genuine warmth, Deganit Nuur and Tim Murphy share accessible daily practices rooted in energy work, intention-setting, and visualization. These thoughtful exercises help realign readers with their sense of purpose, joy, and well-being—making meaningful change feel both realistic and within reach."

——AMY SIKARSKIE, LVN, author, energy therapist, and channeler, host of the *Spirit & Soul Healing Podcast*

"This book is not something you consume—it's something you commune with. *Imagine* invites you into stillness, into presence, into power. It is sacred work. This book meets you exactly where you are, offering practical tools for healing, self-discovery, and connection to something greater than ourselves."

—HAE LEE, Reiki teacher, healer, EMDR therapist, author of *Reiki Illustrated* and founder of STAY+VIBE

"This book is a sacred treasure chest. Deganit and Tim lovingly offer tools that awaken your spirit, align your energy, and expand your joy. A must-read for anyone on a path of heart-led healing."

—AMY LEIGH MERCREE, creator of Atomic Healing™, bestselling author of nineteen books and decks, including *Aura Alchemy* and *The Atomic Element Healing Oracle*

"Deganit is a trusted friend and advisor. Her work is full of magic and integrity, and what she teaches comes from lived experience and a long line of time-tested ancient wisdom."

—DR. JENNIFER FREED, bestselling author of *Use Your Planets Wisely* and *A Map to Your Soul*

"*Imagine* is a clear, powerful guide to awakening your inner strength, peace, and intuition through seven transformative meditations. With simple steps, real-life case studies, and deep insight into why these practices work, this book can shift your sense of Self and the way you create your life. I'm using these meditations—and the results are real. Highly recommended."

—DEBRA LANDWEHR ENGLE, author of *The Only Little Prayer You Need*

"This book gives language to what so many of us feel but don't know how to express. *Imagine* is powerful, practical, and beautifully designed to help you heal from the inside out."

—AMY CHAN, *New York Times* featured author of *Breakup Bootcamp*, relationship expert, and founder of Renew Breakup Bootcamp

"Deganit and Tim have woven ancient metaphysical wisdom with accessible modern practices, creating a framework of visualizations that will help you clear the noise, reconnect with your truth, and confidently command your reality. Whether you're new to energy work or deep into your journey, this book is a powerful ally for becoming more of who you truly are."

—GEORGE LIZOS, bestselling author of *Protect Your Light* and *Ancient Manifestation Secrets*

"Reading *Imagine* felt like a remembering of who I truly am beneath the noise. Deganit and Tim don't just guide you . . . they see you. Their words meet you with warmth, clarity, and the kind of love that gently awakens your spirit."

—JO PLACENCIO, Reiki master, intuitive, Nuurvana graduate, soulful fashionista

IMAGINE

7 Visualizations
for Greater Clarity,
Confidence,
and Calm

Deganit Nuur, DACM, LAc
and Tim Murphy, PhD

Foreword by Anita Moorjani,
bestselling author of *Dying to Be Me*

HAMPTON ROADS

This edition first published in 2025 by
Hampton Roads Publishing, an imprint of

Red Wheel/Weiser, LLC
With offices at:
65 Parker Street, Suite 7
Newburyport, MA 01950

Sign up for our newsletter and special offers by going to *www*
.redwheelweiser.com/newsletter

Material excerpted from *Hafiz's Little Book of Life* © 2023 Erfan Mojib
and Gary Gach published by Hampton Roads Publishing, an imprint of
Red Wheel/Weiser LLC. Newburyport, MA , *www.redwheelweiser.com*.

Cover design by Deganit Nuur
Interior by Maureen Forys, Happenstance Type-O-Rama
Typeset in Sabon, Tenderness, and Montserrat

ISBN: 978-1-64297-074-6

Library of Congress Cataloging-in-Publication Data available upon
request.

Printed in the United States of America
IBI

10 9 8 7 6 5 4 3 2 1

To those who came before us,
Who passed along this infinite wisdom.
And to you, reading this book,
For keeping the power of the imagination alive.

CONTENTS

FOREWORD

Dear Readers,

It is with great pleasure and enthusiasm that I introduce you to the transformative journey that awaits within the pages of *Imagine: 7 Visualizations for Greater Clarity, Confidence, and Calm* by Deganit Nuur and Tim Murphy. As a seeker on the path of self-discovery, healing, and empowerment, I have encountered countless teachings and tools, but something is truly special about the energy tools presented in this book.

Deganit and Tim have masterfully crafted a guide that invites you to embark on a profound exploration of your inner world. The seven energy tools they share are not just concepts, they are gateways to a deeper understanding of yourself and the boundless potential that resides within you. Having experienced these tools firsthand, I can attest to their potency in commanding one's energy field and unlocking the innate wisdom that lies within.

In a world where the metaphysical often seems elusive or abstract, *Imagine* emerges as a grounded and authentic guide in spiritual growth and self-healing. The approach is refreshing, providing a practical and accessible bridge between the mystical and the everyday. It is this grounded perspective that sets *Imagine* apart, offering readers a pathway to navigate the metaphysical realms with confidence and clarity.

The journey outlined in these pages will lead you toward increased authenticity, confidence, and intuition. Through Deganit and Tim's guidance, you will discover how to become the commander of your own life, steering it in the direction of your dreams. As you delve into the wisdom contained within these chapters, you will find yourself equipped with invaluable tools to navigate life's challenges, heal old wounds, and cultivate a profound connection with your innermost self.

I wholeheartedly recommend *Imagine* to my audience and to anyone seeking a grounded approach to the metaphysical world. May this book be a guiding light on your path, illuminating the way to a more authentic, empowered, and intuitive existence.

Wishing you transformative insights and boundless joy on your journey,

ANITA MOORJANI
Bestselling Author of *Dying to Be Me* and *What If This Is Heaven?*

INTRODUCTION

*How often do you overthink, overanalyze,
or become a little obsessive?*

*Do you doubt yourself? Second-guess your actions
or words? Do negative and limiting beliefs
sometimes haunt you?*

*What about feelings of overwhelm?
Do you feel like you can't keep up or have too little
time for yourself? Are you not always able to
identify exactly why you feel overwhelmed?*

*Do you feel burdened by the weight of the world? Are you
having difficulty accepting all that you can't control?*

Ever feel like there has to be more to life than this?

WELCOME. YOU HAVE ARRIVED.

Track your self-assessments online at Nuurvana.com/imagine

IMAGINE A WORLD . . .
where we prioritize ourselves.
where we listen to our gut feelings.
where we are seen, heard, validated, and loved.
where we speak our truth with confidence and ease.
where we feel healed, protected, supported, and cared for.
where we wake up feeling light, hopeful, and fulfilled.
where we manifest the lives our very soul's desire.

Through the simple technique of visualization, applied in seven different ways, you will learn how to transform your life and get your power back.

- The visualizations in this book will help you gain insight into your unconscious patterns, habits, and behaviors so you can acquire a sense of calm, live intentionally, and be your most authentic self.

- Through guided imagery, you will become acquainted with tools that will rewire your brain and nervous system so you fear less and trust more. You will become a friend to yourself so you can get out of your head and into your life.

- You will learn how these visualizations work, be given clear directives on how to use them, and learn about best practices for how to integrate this work into your life for long-lasting results.

What to Expect

On one level, this book is about learning how to be your most authentic self in a world that often makes us feel out of sorts.

On another, this book is a fundamental course in accessing your intuition. The better handle you have on your intuition, the more authentic you are able to be in your walk through life. Here, you will hone your intuition by way of your imagination through guided visualizations.

 Imagination and intuition are
just one frequency apart.

In Part I of the book, "Energetic Awareness," you will learn how to use four different visualization tools that can aid you in better understanding your unique energy. You will learn to distinguish between the energy that is authentically yours and that which you have picked up from other people or environments. You also will learn how to manage your energy so that it works best for you.

In Part II of the book, "Commanding Energy," you will learn how to use three additional visualization tools. You will learn how to command different physical locations to serve your highest purpose, to redistribute energy in order to better tap into your most authentic self, and to manifest the best life that you can imagine for yourself.

Each of the book's seven chapters introduces you to a different tool through a guided visualization and explanation. Each chapter also includes recommendations for real-life situations in which the particular tool will be most useful and effective, case studies that illustrate how it has helped others who have used it, and self-assessments to help you gauge how you are feeling and how the tool is working. You will finish each chapter with a thorough understanding of each tool, including how, when, and why to use it.

How These Tools Helped Us and Others

Hi, New Friend! Welcome. My name is Deganit.

To pronounce my name, just remember the French Impressionist Edgar Degas (*Deg-ah*) who drew the ballerinas. He was pretty *neat*, right? That's me, Deganit (*Deg-ah-NEET*). I am so glad you are you and that you are here to embark on this journey!

As a brown immigrant kid who grew up in public housing with a thick Farsi accent and a bad bowl cut, I started school feeling more than out of place. Throughout my teens and early twenties I was struggling with disordered eating, ADHD, financial insecurity, and indecisiveness. I couldn't pick a lane, whether in terms of my career, my appearance, or my driving (by the time I was twenty-three, I had been in over twenty-three car accidents!).

Growing up, I did my best to win the approval of others. I directed all of my energy into being an overachiever, winning competitive academic awards, perfecting the violin, working at the family business, and helping to raise my baby brother. But no matter how much I achieved, I continued to question my worth.

Thanks to the very tools you are about to learn, I am now a doctor of acupuncture and a clairvoyant intuitive with twenty years of experience helping tens of thousands of people around the world who feel lost, frustrated, and depressed, or who are grappling with uncertainty, anxiety, overwhelm, heartache, disappointment, poor boundaries, and loneliness.

It has become clear to me that experiences of uncertainty and overthinking are extremely pervasive, perhaps more now than ever before. People of all professions and walks of life regularly find themselves caught in turbulent seas of self-doubt, confusing emotions, and overwhelming thoughts.

Take, for example, the coauthor of this book, my bestie, Tim! Tim grew up queer and highly sensitive in a small midwestern city. Despite being blessed with a loving and supportive family, at school, Tim got the memo early that it wasn't a good idea to recognize and accept himself as queer. The more he self-abandoned and compartmentalized his life, the less he got bullied and the better he could fit into his surroundings. Tim found solace in art, music, and his escapes to the local community theater where he could let his imagination run wild with other creatives. Yet, so many years of masking his authenticity resulted in shame, a lack of self-acceptance, and poor self-confidence that persisted throughout his early adulthood.

Not long after Tim and I met twenty years ago, we discovered just how powerful these visualization tools can be as we began using them on our paths to becoming the most authentic version of ourselves. We have been dancing to the tune of our respective truths ever since! The energy tools in this book will help you do the same. You will learn how to silence the energetic noise around you, and soon you, too, will be grooving to your own rhythm!

✴

Welcome, Everyone! I'm Tim.

As Deganit mentioned, growing up as a queer kid in the eighties, I struggled with self-acceptance. Like her, I was very much out of touch with my authenticity as society gave me the impression that it was best to repress core aspects of myself. As I searched for answers, I became fascinated with other cultures and ways of life far from my roots. As a young adult, I traveled widely, taking up residence in Europe and South America, studying language and culture, and eventually developing a fascination for anthropology. Through these experiences, I became more self-confident and accepting of myself.

When Deganit and I met, we were both in a transition period, living with friends and family in a city we barely knew, waiting tables, and preparing for graduate school. The two restaurants we worked at were owned by the same corporation and were separated only by a parking lot. I won a gift card at work for her restaurant and didn't want to waste it, so one day, after my shift, a coworker and I walked across the parking lot to have a drink. Deganit was our server, and it was love (and lots of laughter) at first sight. Within two weeks, Deganit had transferred to work at my restaurant (so we could keep on laughing), and I had given her a pretty radical haircut. We were thick as thieves, and it was during this time that Deganit started learning about these tools and sharing her experience with me.

About a year later, we parted ways to pursue graduate school. I began a PhD program in anthropology in Northern California while Deganit started studying acupuncture in Southern California. Not long after beginning my program, my self-confidence quickly deteriorated, causing me much anxiety, self-doubt, and a general sense of overwhelm. Deganit and I kept in close touch during this time apart, and she began teaching me some of the intuitive tools laid out in this book over the phone.

I went on to implement them as I navigated graduate study, teaching, and my personal relationships. I had lots of questions for Deganit as I started out, which resulted in many fruitful discussions over the phone between the two of us. We were both very much still students of these tools, so we were learning and deepening our relationship with this work through these conversations. In fact, these conversations became the inspiration for writing this book.

Ever since, I have been hooked on using these tools in my daily life. I have regained my self-confidence, my anxiety has diminished, and I understand myself much better.

My training as an anthropologist has helped me tremendously with these tools. Let me explain.

First of all, broadly speaking, cultural anthropologists like myself study the belief systems, practices, and social organizations of human cultures. To do so, we immerse ourselves in the cultures we study for extended periods, which often means learning the language and engaging in the daily activities.

The basic idea underpinning this approach is that we can best understand what others' lives are like by putting ourselves in their shoes. Yet when we do so, we don't automatically forget what it felt like to have our own shoes on. In other words, our personal perspectives and assumptions can easily creep in when we're trying to understand the cultures and life ways of others. Therefore anthropologists have to learn to be open, neutral, and as free of any judgment as possible when we conduct research so that our own values and biases don't compromise our ability to understand the people we are studying.

Because humans are naturally biased, staying open and neutral can be challenging. Some anthropologists try to be as neutral as possible by opening up all of our senses, paying close attention, and simply witnessing what we observe. Rather than going in with assumptions or quickly jumping to conclusions, our job is to stay open and pay attention. The point isn't for us to determine what we think is right or wrong, good or bad. Rather, we try to understand. It's about allowing whatever we see, hear, or feel, to just be, whatever it is.

Much of the work you will do in this book involves taking a similar approach. Only rather than observing another culture, you will be observing images that appear in your mind while Deganit guides you through the visualization exercises.

This will be especially true in the first part of the book, "Energetic Awareness," where you are encouraged to allow whatever comes up to just be and to try your best to accept whatever you observe. Here is where seeing like an anthropologist comes in handy. Try your best to stay open to what you observe so you can understand rather than evaluate. As best as you can, allow and accept whatever arises without judgment.

These tools are almost like a new language that you will quickly learn and practice in your mind with your eyes closed. To me, this space feels like another world from the one we normally operate in with our eyes open. By entering into another language and world of visuals to do this work, we are able to gain a certain distance from our egos and our personal biases, which can help us better understand and heal without the limiting baggage and judgment we often unconsciously carry.

As you continue to learn these tools, try to see like an anthropologist—remain open, curious, and attentive to whatever arises.

What Each Tool Offers

Most of the tools in this book are helpful in multiple ways: to get your power back, to increase self-love and self-acceptance, to build self-confidence, and to become acquainted with your own light. Here is a list of what each tool excels at:

- The Golden Sun tool helps you regain your personal power.
- The Grounding Cord tool helps you release unwanted energy.
- The Separation tool helps you maintain boundaries.

- The Center of Your Head tool helps you achieve an elevated perspective.
- The Grounding Locations tool helps you experience a sense of belonging.
- The Creation/Destruction tool helps you clear energy blocks.
- The Manifestation tool helps you actualize your pure potential.

Rather than a cognitive practice, this is an intuitive journey. By imagining and visualizing, you will learn how to encounter your answers in a trance state, not a waking one. You will learn to drop into this state with the snap of your fingers and begin to incorporate this new skill into your daily life, at work, on the bus, and eventually, possibly, even mid-conversation with coworkers, partners, and family members.

Informed by neuroplasticity, limbic resonance, psychology, metaphysics, and anthropology, these tools will show you who you are, helping you to believe in and trust yourself. We hope to empower and inspire you on your own journey toward greater clarity, peace, belonging, and certainty.

Noise versus Truth

Hey, it's me, Deganit!

Ever since I was a child, I have been sensitive to energetic noise, only I haven't always understood what that means. I started kindergarten in the US speaking very little English, and I was the only brown kid in my class. This formative experience instilled within me a sensation of not belonging, which continued into my adulthood. I became consumed with what other people seemed to like, and the goals they had or how they presented themselves, almost as if I was studying a foreign species that I could imitate in hopes of feeling included.

What ended up happening is that I ignored my inner voice and neglected my own desires while I pretended to like the same things that all the other students in my class seemed to like. Whether it was French braids, fruit juices, or favorite books, if *they* liked it, I liked it. My entire personality and identity was a reaction to my environment. The outside voices became my inner voice . . . and my true inner voice seemed to vanish. For our purposes, let's call these outside voices *noise* and our true inner voice the *truth*.

As a kid, I wanted so desperately to belong that I would unknowingly swap out my truth for noise all the time in my constant quest for approval. My youngest brother was born when I was nine, and that is when I took on the role of a parent. I fed my two brothers, helped them with homework, put the youngest to bed, and tended to all matters of the home before diving into my studies, making sure I maintained my high GPA. As an unskilled intuitive unconsciously taking on the struggle of my elders, I wanted nothing more than to show them that their plight wasn't in vain. So I set out to do what any good Iranian Jewish daughter would do: fulfill the immigrant dream of becoming a medical professional. I convinced myself I wanted to become a dentist (talk about noise clouding my truth!).

The saying, "rejection is the universe's protection" could not have been more accurate in my case. After graduating college, I applied to dental school and got rejected. I was devastated and determined to get in the following year, which is why I moved to California's Central Valley to live with a friend from college and work at a test prep center for the Dental Admissions Test. I worked as a dental assistant by day, waited tables by night, and taught aspiring dentists on the weekends. Although I thought I had moved there to increase my chances of getting into dental school, I quickly learned that was all noise. What was revealed instead was my truth.

As Tim mentioned, it was during that year that we met and I first learned about the tools presented in this book. I was recovering from a decade of bulimia, adamant about dentistry, head-over-heels in love with a woman, yet closeted to my family, and just generally neglecting my authenticity. I was living a lie, only I didn't know it until one of my coworkers, Kayhan Ghodsi, gave me my first intuitive reading. Although what he said felt worlds away from who I was at the time, it resonated so deeply that I was eager to learn anything he had to offer me. This coworker, moonlighting as a skilled intuitive and energy worker, quickly became my teacher.

He introduced me to these energy tools and taught me their history—most importantly, that they have been used globally for thousands of years. In the 1970s, a man named Lewis S. Bostwick traveled the world to study common metaphysical practices in indigenous cultures and noticed an overlap of energy tools and modalities used. He simplified and condensed the overlap into what would later become the curriculum of the Berkeley Psychic Institute, which is where my teacher studied. Bostwick's dream was for these tools to spread far and wide, transforming lives and ultimately elevating the consciousness of our collective. And this leads us to where we are now, humbled to be carrying out his mission, as world peace through inner peace is our dream too.

After just a few weeks of intuitive training using these tools to connect with my authenticity and gain clarity and a sense of calm, I began testing out my intuition by reading my friends. In fact, Tim was the very first recipient of my burgeoning skills! Being the curious anthropologist that he is, his interest and intrigue offered me the subconscious permission I needed to explore my intuition.

Practicing these tools helped me shed layers of noise, programming, and "shoulds" while more deeply connecting me with my authenticity and intuition. I was showing up for life in ways I had never dared to before! When Tim suggested a faux-hawk-long-layered-mullet for me, I was overcome with excitement and tickled by the idea! Finally, for the first time, my initial reaction wasn't "what will people think?"

That radical haircut only expanded and amplified my spiritual growth journey. I was stuck with a haircut that required a lot of confidence, as it drew a lot of attention. Not only was I learning how to access my truth, the haircut helped me *own* my truth. Before I knew it, this hobby of doing intuitive readings was bringing in more income than my job waiting tables. Rather than my friends dismissing me, as I expected, they pointed out my high level of accuracy and encouraged me to consider that this just might be my calling.

I traded in dentistry for acupuncture and clairvoyant healing—offering readings and teaching these tools to clients and students to pay my way. I haven't looked back once. The readings put me through graduate school, which is where my classmates asked me to teach them all that I knew. This was the impetus for the intuitive training program I later developed, which was based on Tim's own intuitive training. And now here the two of us are, putting together what we have learned into a book for you.

Now back to the topic of noise versus truth:

What I mean by noise might be better understood as energetic background noise—energy that is not actually yours but that creeps in and distracts you nonetheless.

When matter is broken down into its smallest particles, everything is energy, and energy is in constant motion. Even though Earth appears still, it is in constant motion. As is our own energy and the energy in our environment. As a result, at any given moment, even if we can't see it, we are exchanging energies with our surroundings—we breathe one another's air and dance with one another's frequencies.

Science is able to measure our electromagnetic fields. Did you know that the electromagnetic field of your heart expands around you by approximately four feet? Truly astonishing, and yet ancient mystics have known this all along and most commonly refer to this energy field as your aura. The more in-tune you get with your own energy field, the better you are able to discern what is yours and what is not yours.

Let us give you an example where you can practice a little imagining:

To keep it simple, let's refer to your energy as *your truth* and let's pretend your truth is the color purple. Let's label anything that is not yours as *noise* and pretend that noise is the color green.

Now, imagine an average weekday morning in which you are commuting to work on a crowded subway. It is likely that you are standing within the electromagnetic fields of three to four other people. Without most people realizing it, they are taking on your purple, and you are taking on their various greens. There could be equal parts green noise in your energetic space as there is purple truth, but if you are unaware of this distinction, you will likely not realize that the green noise isn't yours. You may think everything in your space actually belongs to you and recognize the green noise as your truth.

Perhaps the person beside you is running late and is terribly nervous about it; their green nervous energy is in your energetic space. What if the person across from you is going through a breakup? Now their green heartbreak energy is in your purple space, as well. The person behind you has a newborn and hardly got any sleep last night; their green exhaustion and frustration energy is also taking up residence in your energy field. It is entirely possible that with this many people surrounding you, your space has more green noise than purple truth. Of course, few people are consciously aware of energy at work in this way.

For example, you could be feeling the green anxiety-heartbreak-exhaustion energy and dismissing it entirely by thinking, "I don't know why I am feeling this way. I woke up happy, and my life is going great both personally and professionally. I'll just ignore this feeling." But ignoring the green noise doesn't make it go away, and now it is taking up precious real estate in your space and crowding out your purple truth.

Imagine you have a presentation to give today, and even though you have been certain of your message for a solid week, you are suddenly doubting yourself. Maybe it was that guy standing next to you who, unbeknownst to you, was running late and hates his job. His energy coursed through your system and left you feeling less enthusiastic and confident than normal. The presentation goes okay, but you leave feeling a little off because there is noise in your space that is competing with your truth. But you have a board meeting to get to, so you don't think much about it and just keep moving along. Then, you suddenly get a news alert on your phone about a tragedy, yet before you have a chance to read about it, a friend in crisis texts you asking if you have time to talk. And just like that, you are overwhelmed, having accepted the noise as a part of you.

Our hope is that once you realize the green is not yours, you will be better able to release all that noise and become more in tune with your truth. In doing so, you can witness the news and be a good friend without getting derailed.

Before we began practicing these tools, we easily mistook the green noise as our truth because it was in our respective energetic spaces. We had never functioned exclusively from our own energy, so we did not know our respective truths—what they feel, look, and act like.

This takes the phrase, "we are products of our environment" to a whole new level. As you practice the tools introduced in this book, take some time to see how you feel in the presence of different people in your life. It is likely that with some you feel more confident, whereas with others you feel shyer; some people may bring out the inner critic in you, while others inspire your inner cheerleader. Start observing yourself—your inner landscape and your outward actions and behaviors—to cultivate self-awareness and gain a deeper understanding of your truth.

 Once you are able to distinguish your truth from the noise, you will be better able to amplify your truth and tune out the noise.

Before learning these energy tools, I would wake up feeling great, and then throughout my day, my mood would change depending on my environment. I remember that during high school, my mood would change from class to class. In French I was cheery, in Geometry I was sad. I would get so down on myself. But why? What was wrong with me? I was excelling at both subjects, had friends in both classes, and had no reason for the contrast in my feelings. I would then go into History class, and again my mood would change. Just like that, I would become defensive and crass in the presence of a group of bullies who sat near me. It was puzzling to me, and I found the rapid fluctuation of moods, thoughts, and physiological sensations very disempowering.

I was convinced that I was emotionally unstable and concerned that I was not cut out for this life. But it was my environment that was controlling me, and I didn't even know it.

Rather than being intentional with the energy in my life, at that point I was a sponge for all the different energies coming in and was completely unaware of their impact on me. But now, thanks to these tools, I am able to both command my own energy with intention and better recognize the noise for what it is and even find value in it. You will too!

Within the first year of practicing these tools I felt emotionally stable for the first time in my life. My confidence grew, my friendships evolved, and my path unfolded in the most beautiful and synergistic ways. These tools have changed my life, and it is my greatest honor to share them with you. Our wish for you is the same wish we have for all who practice these tools: that you gain mental freedom, emotional well-being, self-confidence, and authenticity.

We were fortunate to have found these tools early in our adult lives. They have become even more helpful as I have aged into greater responsibilities and higher stakes. In 2012, I fulfilled a childhood fantasy of mine and created a multidisciplinary healing center, employing brilliant clairvoyant intuitives. At its prime, the center had eight practitioners and hosted regular healing circles, full-moon rituals, and other metaphysical events. The reception area was like a living room, facilitating the beginning of many beautiful friendships and even a few romantic relationships.

I used these tools when I hired my team, while guiding clients, teaching classes, negotiating contracts, being interviewed, managing health scares, tending to family matters, dealing with legal issues, and more. Given all the difficult stories I often hear from clients, I believe that had these tools not become habits, I would have been vulnerable to depression within my first few weeks of working. Tim has also felt their impact as he has shared these tools in mindfulness workshops with professors and students and as he regularly uses them so he can be of service to all those in need.

These tools have taken care of us so that we are better able to take care of others while maintaining our own inner peace and joy. By operating from your own authenticity, you, too, will be more effective at helping others and making the world a better place.

 You are the expert in you.

Making the Tools Your Own

Your first-hand experience with these tools will cultivate your own personal relationship with them and allow you to collect your own empirical data. We are not advocates of blind faith and believe that, especially with this kind of work, only you know what is best for you. The proof is in the pudding, so rather than taking our word for it, please experience the efficacy of these tools for yourselves and make them your own. Rather than attempting to provide you with some external universal truth for you to follow, this book intends to provide you with a roadmap for how to discover and honor *your truth*. This offering of visualization tools will help you get in better touch with your intuition, your highest self, and your unique purpose and path.

This book can be used in a few different ways. We recommend one of the following:

- Focus on one lesson per week and spend the week practicing it.
- Read the entire book at once, and then go back and take your time practicing the tools.
- Go at whatever pace feels right for you and return to the lessons and practice them at any time.

Remember, ultimately, you are the expert in you. Although these tools offer you the structure and framework with which to hone your intuition, we leave room for you and your personal preferences. Customize the tools and make them your own.

❋

You are the gift. Once you find your balance, you will embody the tools. They will change your biochemistry and become a part of you. *You* are the point of this book. The tools are just the path to you.

Everyone has a unique experience with these tools. Some readers will find certain tools easy to work with and others more difficult. Others may have difficulty visualizing anything at all and will need to trust the fundamental truths behind this entire process: *Energy follows intention and practice makes permanent.*

Because these tools are mastered experientially, if you ever find yourself overanalyzing, drifting off, disconnecting, judging, or dismissing the material, then it is time to take a break. In general, however, most readers will notice almost immediate results—feeling calmer, grounded, and in touch with their highest selves after completing a lesson. You can use the self-assessments toward the beginning and end of each chapter to see for yourself how they are working.

As you practice these tools, try to take note of subtle shifts taking place in your life—for example, maybe a coworker is being more friendly to you than normal, you experience a stroke of good luck, or you just get a general feeling of synchronicity. Please also be aware that when working with the metaphysical, healing is not linear, and you may experience unexpected waves of expansion and contraction. Try to remain open and expect the unexpected.

Please also note that this book is not meant to replace other mental and medical healthcare approaches like seeing a therapist or consulting your primary healthcare practitioner. May these tools serve as a complement to your lifestyle and spiritual or religious beliefs and reinforce the benefits of the other healing modalities you are utilizing.

Foundational Assumptions

By working together as teacher and student, and through our many conversations over the years, we have become aware of a few assumptions that underpin the method outlined in the coming chapters. The more that readers are able to accept these five assumptions, the more they will be able to benefit from this book. After completing the lessons, we think you will agree.

1. We each have a unique spiritual path worthy of honor and discovery.

2. To uncover our unique spiritual paths, we must look inward for answers rather than outward.

3. We are here to focus on the light.

4. Each of us is an active participant in our own destiny.

5. Loving and accepting oneself is fundamental to spiritual growth.

Let's Imagine Together!

PART I
ENERGETIC
AWARENESS

1

Regaining Your Power:
Golden Sun Tool

The town is empty of love
Until one person
Acts beyond their self.
—HAFIZ

Energetic Awareness

You are energy! You know this, right? You probably learned it in science class in elementary school, but like so many of us, you either quickly forgot it or just don't have it at the forefront of your mind as you go through your average day. This book helps you develop greater awareness of your energy and use this awareness to improve your daily life.

When we develop greater awareness of our energy, it becomes easier for us to understand how we are feeling and where those feelings are coming from. This awareness can also help us get to the root of why we are thinking about a particular topic and what we can do with such thoughts when they are not serving us.

One of the easiest ways to begin understanding our own energy is by harnessing our own personal power. We all have power. Our bodies run on our power, and we draw on it to accomplish all kinds of tasks, whether mundane or complex. We use our power to breathe air, to get out of bed, to eat and digest food, and to engage in conversations with others.

We also use large amounts of our power to study for tests, to try to come up with solutions to complicated problems, to stand up for ourselves and for others, and to worry about virtually everything under the sun. Because Western society doesn't prioritize energetic awareness over other types of knowing, most of us are largely unaware of how our personal power is affected by our daily walk through life. For example,

- Have you ever thought you were having a pretty good day or week and then have suddenly found yourself in a bad mood, worrying, overthinking, or feeling discouraged and haven't known exactly why?

- Have you ever felt confused about your feelings of loneliness or emptiness? Have you ever felt overwhelmed or discouraged by those feelings?

- Have you ever felt like you are running on empty? Depleted, yet anxious at the same time?

Rest assured, the Golden Sun tool is here to save the day! This chapter introduces you to your Golden Sun, which will help you develop awareness of your personal power and teach you how to regain the power that you expend during an average day.

Here are some times and situations in which you might want to use the Golden Sun tool. At the beginning of each chapter, you'll see a similar list for each tool.

GOLDEN SUN AS MEDICINE	GOLDEN SUN AS RITUAL
When you can't get out of bed	First thing in the morning
When you are tired, pissed, and overwhelmed by it all	Before you look at your phone, engage with the world, or begin your morning commute
When you are feeling lonely or hollow (read: dead) on the inside	Every time you shower (Imagine the water as Golden Sun energy filling you in.)
During a midday slump	When you put on your sunglasses (Did someone say Sun?)
When you swear everyone else has it better than you	Before, during, and after scrolling through news and social media
When you just can't	After your workday or daily commute
When you need your power back	Before bed

In just a moment, you will be guided through the steps for the Golden Sun tool. Before you begin, take a moment to assess how you are feeling right now.

SELF-ASSESSMENT

Ask yourself the following questions. On a scale of 1 to 5:

_____   *How energetic am I feeling right now?* (Where 1 is "Lethargic. I feel like a sloth," and 5 is "I feel refreshed like after a good night's sleep.")

_____   *How empowered am I feeling right now?* (Where 1 is "I feel like my life is not my own," and 5 is "I'm capable of anything. I've got this!")

_____   *How authentic am I feeling right now?* (Where 1 is "I'm confused about who I am and what I want," and 5 is "I feel aligned with my true purpose.")

_____   *How present am I feeling right now?* (Where 1 is "I'm not sure how it's possible, but I'm both future tripping and dwelling on the past at the same time," and 5 is "This moment is all I've got. I'm right here right now.")

Visualizing

In a moment, you will allow your eyes to close and look within. Start slowing down your breath to begin box breathing as described here.

Inhale for four counts, then hold your breath for four counts, then exhale for four counts, and then hold for four counts. Repeat. Inhale for 4, 3, 2, 1; hold for 4, 3, 2, 1; exhale for 4, 3, 2, 1; hold for 4, 3, 2, 1.

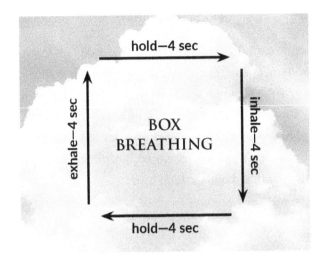

Imagine, about two feet above your head, a huge, radiant Golden Sun is attracting all your own personal power and life force energy and directing it back to you. Anything you may have lost throughout the day through interactions, conversations, and thoughts is now pouring back into your Golden Sun, filling it up with bright gold light.

Your Power, Your Name

In the center of this Golden Sun is a magnet in the shape of your name; it magnetizes all your gold light as it comes back into your Golden Sun. Watch as the gold light fills your Golden Sun all the way up. Gold light represents self-healing energy. This energy is the energy that works best for you.

If you haven't already done so, go ahead and close your eyes and visualize your Golden Sun.

Watch as your Golden Sun calls all your golden light energy back from places in the past or in the future where you may have left your gold light, whether through interactions, events, thoughts, or simple awareness.

Watch as gold light comes into your Golden Sun from objects that you touched throughout the day. Observe all of that gold leaving your wallet, your phone, and your keys as it pours back into your Golden Sun. Watch as any energy left behind in events, activities, people, places, or experiences comes pouring back into your Golden Sun.

Now look up at your Golden Sun and notice how shiny, bright, and full it is! It has filtered out any energy that is not yours and set your energy to the current time and space so it can best serve you right here and now. Your Golden Sun is so full that it looks like it is ready to burst. Do you see it?

Intention Setting

Great! Now, before you bring all your Golden Sun energy into your body to revitalize and nourish yourself, you can go ahead and set an intention for this energy. This step is not required but can be helpful when you want your energy to be in alignment with a particular purpose. Picture whatever intention you wish to vibrate from written clearly on your Golden Sun in the present tense. "I am at peace," "I feel worthy," "I am healthy," "I feel confident," and so on. Whatever your intention is, see it beaming back at you and know that it is doing its work and setting the vibration of every energetic particle in your Golden Sun to this exact message.

Filling Up

All right, now poke a hole in the bottom of your Golden Sun and let all that beautiful, golden light into your body. It is coming in from the very top of your head and falling directly down to your toes, filling you up from toe to head, just like when you're filling up a glass with a pitcher of water. Feel the gold light as it fills up your feet and ankles. Watch as the gold light fills up your shins, calves, knees, and every single tendon, bone, ligament, and muscle in your legs.

This gold light continues to fill you up, coming up your thighs and into your hips, lower back, and lower stomach. The light continues to pour in, filling up your entire torso, all your internal organs, your chest and back, shoulders, arms, forearms, hands, palms, and fingers. The light continues up your neck, face, and head so that every single cell in your body is functioning off your own light and personal power. You are feeling fully refreshed and revitalized, fulfilled, excited, and inspired.

Now start wiggling your fingers and toes and allow your eyes to gently flutter open.

＊

When Tim first learned the Golden Sun tool, he loved it so much that he would imagine himself walking around his neighborhood with his Golden Sun hovering above his head. It was kind of hilarious. I remember he told me, "It's like my Golden Sun is my new secret buddy bopping around with me, helping me to stand up straight and lead with confidence!"

I explained to him that there was, in fact, some meaning that he could glean from his unique experience with the Golden Sun. What could his desire to have it hover over his head mean? With practice, Tim eventually learned that being in alignment with his personal power was such an unfamiliar sensation for him at the time that he would get stuck on that first step—envisioning the Golden Sun above his head. Completing all of the steps would suggest that he was ready to accept his personal power and stand in alignment with it.

He had just finished getting his PhD, and graduate school had made him hypercritical of everything, including himself. "I guess it's par for the course." I remember him telling me. "As anthropologists in training, we were reading lots of critical theory and deconstructing the world around us, analyzing virtually anything and everything. In hindsight, it's easy for me to understand how this tendency could negatively impact a person's self-image."

After graduate school was over, Tim was ready to rebuild his self-confidence, and the Golden Sun tool was the answer. Over time, it's gotten easier and easier for him. Each time he fills up with a Golden Sun, he quickly feels replenished and more confident than with it just hovering over his head. "It has also helped me feel less depleted by those around me," he has explained.

When we are consistently using our Golden Suns, we attract more of what sets our souls on fire. These days, Tim knows this to be true, so he tends to fill up with a Golden Sun whenever he's feeling a bit off.

"It's such a quick way to be able to check in with yourself and give back to yourself," Tim attests. "At the very least, I do them at the end of each day before going to bed, which helps me feel centered and prepared for a good night of sleep."

Noticing

Everyone's experience of these tools is completely unique. Just as Tim did with his hovering Golden Sun, what's most important is that you take notice of what comes up for you and trust in the process.

At the beginning, many students have very literal/rational questions about the tools. For example: What happens to the membrane of the Golden Sun after it empties out and fills up your body? Does it also turn into liquid and fill you up? Or does an empty Golden Sun remain above your head?

It's very normal to have such questions because we are used to thinking with the rational part of our brains rather than with our intuition. With practice, these kinds of technical questions will gain less and less importance because at the end of the day, these are just tools to help you hone your energetic awareness and can be manipulated however you like. That said, especially for beginners, it is usually recommended that they visualize the entire Golden Sun—membrane and all—turning into gold liquid and filling up the body.

Energy Follows Intention

One of the most important phrases to remember as you develop your energetic awareness through these tools is *energy follows intention*. For most students, this can take a while to sink in, but with practice, they come to accept "I'm intending it; therefore, I'm doing it."

In other words, try to allow yourself to let go of getting it right or being too literal about these visualizations. Just stay on the path and start to trust more in the process; trust is key. Self-trust begets self-confidence.

Trusting that the Golden Sun will fill you up with your energy and help you regain your personal power is at the root of it all. At first, many people don't see much at all when they close their eyes. When I started doing visualizations, I would often see gray, blurry images, or sometimes quick flashes of images. Sometimes, I would get so relaxed that I would drift off to sleep!

It's important not to get frustrated or impatient when these things happen. *All* of this counts as doing the work. Energy absolutely follows intention. What's important is to keep practicing and trusting that it is working. Practice makes permanent! So regardless of what students see, we remind them that Golden Suns are great to utilize when they're feeling sluggish, defeated, vulnerable, or a little spiritually weak. Golden Suns are great for restoring self-confidence and authenticity and are all-around excellent for self-healing and revitalizing.

Many of us have perfectionist tendencies and can become a little overzealous to get it right when we learn something new. We just have to keep reminding ourselves that the thing with self-discovery is that you really can't get it wrong! We invite students to simply take notice and observe their Golden Suns. Be curious. Ask your Golden Sun, for example, *Why is the size of the Golden Sun that I am visualizing right now the perfect size for me today?* and trust whatever comes up.

Intuition works great with questions. Questions have long been used as powerful divination tools. As you are asking questions, you are focusing your energy, so energy can communicate back to you with clarity and precision. Use these energy tools as an opportunity to both heal and learn about yourself!

Case Study

Brice—From People-Pleasing to Self-Prioritizing

People-pleasing was a part of Brice's identity and a bargaining tool he used in exchange for attention. He also used it to escape from his own personal problems. The truth was, he was feeling very alone, and as long as he had other people's problems to take care of, he didn't have to focus on his own feelings. The people-pleasing was disguised as friendship, which offered him the illusion of being connected. It reinforced the notion of conditional love and worth for Brice—the attention he received was based on the condition that he prioritized others above himself.

We determined that Brice needed to perform Golden Suns at the start of every day and especially when doing things for himself. He needed to learn that he could also benefit from putting himself first and taking care of his own needs. So, to help him, we coupled self-prioritizing with Golden Suns. Brice also began to give himself Golden Suns when he was feeling lonely. Basically, we utilized Golden Suns as a cure-all . . . Because they kind of are.

Brice began to experience increased self-awareness. He was astonished by how often he felt lonely. He wasn't aware that his loneliness was the root of his people-pleasing until it was pointed out. He also started realizing that the people-pleasing made him feel less connected, *not* more connected. Sure, it was nice to receive praise for being of service, but at the end of the day, it started to feel inauthentic and like an empty exchange. Brice began questioning whether people liked him for himself or whether they just liked what he could do for them. He took some time to reexamine his relationships and face his loneliness. With his newfound free time, he started dating! He also started offering himself more unconditional love. He realized he was people-pleasing to feel like he was a good person, and when he didn't do as much for others, he didn't feel as good about himself. Brice realized that this outlook was not helpful, and he is now prioritizing self-care and feeling really good about himself.

USING THE GOLDEN SUN TOOL

Now take a moment to close your eyes and try to visualize the steps of the Golden Sun tool on your own.

Step 1: Imagine a bright Golden Sun hovering two feet above your head.

Step 2: Visualize your name in the center of the Golden Sun.

Step 3: Watch as the Golden Sun fills all the way up with gold light, representing all your own energy.

Step 4: Once the Golden Sun is full, poke a hole in the bottom of it and watch as its liquid fills you up from toe to head.

Good Intentions

When first becoming acquainted with the Golden Sun tool, students often wonder about the intention-setting part. "Are all intentions okay?" they ask. All positive affirmations are great—"I am safe," "All is well in my world," and "I feel loved" are good ones. The trick is to keep intentions/affirmations in the present tense in order to experience the effects in the present moment.

This kind of intention setting is rooted in neuro-linguistic programming (NLP). NLP suggests that if we conceive of something in the future tense, it will indefinitely exist in the future of our minds. That is to say, an intention set in the future tense may feel unattainable and be disempowering. A different cascade of chemical reactions occurs when we say, "I am happy" versus when we say, "I want to be happy," or "I am going to be happy." "I *am* happy" shifts our perspective so that we are happy now exactly as we are, rather than yearning for happiness at some future date.

This is why it is especially important to be mindful of the words we use. People's wants and future-oriented language in particular suggest a lack or a deficiency, whereas words in the present tense can empower us. For example, our brain responds to the sentence "I want *x*" as though we are yearning for something; we anticipate yearning for it indefinitely. "I have" and "I am" statements are a whole different ball game. Because they are in the present tense, they suggest that we are already fulfilled. What's so cool about the Golden Sun tool is that it is always at your disposal to get you powerfully present. It helps you arrive here and receive the present moment as the gift that it is.

Language shapes our reality. Linguists and anthropologists explain how this happens at the level of culture. The Swiss linguist Ferdinand de Saussure basically argued that the language we use influences how we think, see, and behave in the world, ultimately creating what we call *reality*. Without language, the world/our existence would have no meaning whatsoever.

This is pretty mind-blowing when you stop and think about it. But it's obvious when, for example, you know another language and come upon a word that can't be perfectly translated, or if you've experienced immersing yourself in a different language and culture so much that you begin to see things from a different perspective.

Another example of this is when college students take their first cultural anthropology course and are blown away by the idea that the Inuit have more than fifty different names for snow. This fact illustrates how we cocreate reality with our environment. If we live in a place where it snows all the time, snow is more likely to take up a bigger role in our daily life and shape how we see the world.

If language shapes reality, it only makes sense to be intentional about what we say and the kinds of intentions we set for ourselves in order to create the reality that works best for us!

Case Study

Mila—From Accommodating to Aligning

Mila would do anything to hold onto a relationship, even if it meant self-sacrificing. Normally someone who goes to bed early, Mila would stay up late if her partner stayed up late. If he was on a plant-based diet, she would be as well. Mila was overrun by fears of abandonment. It's all she could think about, and that's what she would unconsciously filter her partner's actions through: *Does this behavior indicate he's about to leave me, or is he staying?* She would shift and morph into whatever she assumed her partner wanted. This was her way of feeling safe and secure in relationships. Needless to say, it was an exhausting pattern that left Mila feeling more and more abandoned with time—abandoned by herself especially.

Mila gave herself a few Golden Suns every time she wanted to reach out to her partner. She gave herself Golden Suns every time she wanted to manipulate any arrangement between herself and others, and each time she thought, *I wonder what* xx *thinks of me.* She kept on giving herself Golden Suns until her outward-focused thoughts passed.

At first, Mila was disappointed to find out that, in many cases, if she didn't keep the communication going, it would stop. She felt insignificant to her partner and friends. She went through an awakening of sorts in which she realized the truth of what her relationships really were. She saw her relationship patterns more clearly and how they were also ruining her friendships because she would frequently lean on her friends for moral support. She broke up with her partner and decided to give more to her friendships. Her friendships improved, her self-confidence improved, and Mila felt worthy while single!

Truth versus Noise

Your Golden Sun will help you attract what is most beneficial for you in particular because it fills you up with your own personal power. Your Golden Sun represents your truth, and the more truth is in your space, the less space the energy that is not yours—what we call *noise*—is able to take up.

Believe it or not, many of us have only ever felt and been fueled by the noise that surrounds us. Noise ultimately lowers a person's vibration and increases their confusion because it is not meant for them. The best energy for each person is their own source energy, their truth, which they can access through the Golden Sun. Their energy raises their vibration and confidence. They feel and know who they are and recognize that they belong. Since they are being fueled by their own energy, their life starts to affirm their presence.

We leave our energy behind in conversations and interactions with people and in what we hear, see, and read. We even throw our energy way out into the future with plans, goals, and fears. Sometimes this manifests as *cyclical thinking*, where we find that we repeat the same conversations to ourselves or can't stop obsessing over something that hasn't even happened. They say anxiety is what occurs when our energy is trapped in the future, like when we have worry thoughts and "what ifs." Depression, on the other hand, tends to represent energy trapped in the past, like when we obsess about the glory days of the past when we had it all.

When deploying your Golden Sun, you are calling back pieces of you. When you are the most authentically you, you can feel connected to all that you are! It is like coming home to yourself.

After filling up with Golden Suns on a regular basis, students of these tools often notice how many of their thoughts and actions are inspired by people-pleasing or the desire to control a situation. For example, for people who have difficulty saying no to people's requests, saying yes often seems like the right thing to do. But this can quickly produce feelings of burden and even resentment toward the people making the request. Doing Golden Suns regularly can help us better evaluate if we want to say yes or no to a request and more confidently honor whichever answer surfaces. This in turn helps us be more authentic, honor our thoughts and actions, and share our true selves. We stop committing to things out of a sense of obligation, and instead, we begin saying yes to what makes us enthusiastic about life. Aligning yourself with your real values and priorities instead of living life on autopilot and simply going through the motions can feel almost euphoric.

Case Study

Pauline—From Feeling Spent to Feeling Supported

Pauline does it all! She cooks, she cleans, she parents, she partners, but who is there for Pauline? Pauline begged her husband for more support; she expressed to him how frustrated she was, how tired she was, how she felt like an only parent, and although her husband seemed to sympathize, he just didn't seem to get it. She felt disappointed in him and resentful. If she was being honest, she was resentful of a lot of people. She was tired and wanted help. The assistance she did receive seemed to always fall short, leaving Pauline to believe if she wanted something done right, she had to do it herself. Thus, her resentment grew.

Golden Suns for all! Previously, Pauline was showing up for her kids more than she was for herself, so this tool could be used to everyone's advantage. Pauline shared the Golden Sun tool with her children. She didn't think it would resonate because they were still so young, but it did! Children are closer to cosmic consciousness than adults are, and so they often heal, shift, and ascend faster than we do. Pauline's kids would giggle any time she would wave her imaginary wand and gift them a Golden Sun. She would giggle when they would gift her a Golden Sun. It became part of their family language. Any time someone was grouchy, the whole family would gift them a Golden Sun. If one of them was tired, cranky, sleepy, crying, angry—anything less than in their power—the entire family would play Golden Sun Time.

Pauline felt so loved and supported by her kids and by her Golden Sun! Golden Sunning through diaper changes, making meals, and all the mundane things that she had previously resented soon reminded her that her life was something she had once wished for. She started remembering what a blessing her "problems" were. She felt more connected to her children— like they were all in this together rather than feeling like the only one holding down the fort. She realized she wasn't a victim at all; her life was going exactly as she wanted. That shift in perspective made all the difference!

When fully in her power, Pauline stopped cooking when she didn't want to. The family would order in on those nights. She stopped cleaning when she didn't want to. As it turns out, her husband does know how to clean after all! She had just kept beating him to the punch. In short, Pauline now only gives from a place of overflow, not depletion. She's more energized and enthusiastic by the day.

Color

People sometimes ask questions about the color of the Golden Sun: *Why gold and not a different-colored sun? Is there any spiritual significance to the sun being gold? Would a pink or a white sun not be as effective?*

Generally speaking, gold light represents neutrality and self-healing. So this is the color that gets you back to you, reinforces your truth and personal power, and starts you healing yourself. It's kind of like when we accidentally cut ourselves; our body just knows how to heal. It's the same with Golden Sun energy.

   Golden Sun energy knows what you need and will offer you exactly that.

Each color carries its own vibration and frequency. White tends to resonate with the spiritual realm. It can represent ascension and growth. It's not exactly bad to fill up with a White Sun, but the thing about a Golden Sun is that it lifts you to white-energy consciousness. You can think of it this way: Gold helps you achieve heaven on Earth, whereas white represents heaven and can sometimes help you escape Earth. White is not as grounding as gold. Meanwhile, silver is often used to depict angelic energy. You may not want to fill up with energy that's not yours—even if it is angelic. You are still in human form, so what will help your body best is your own gold light.

Frequency

The frequency with which you engage your Golden Sun depends on what feels best for you. For most people, it depends on the day. I give myself a Golden Sun in between sessions with clients, and generally every time I finish any type of meeting. Also, I realize that when I'm feeling a little crabby or judgy, it indicates that I'm feeling crowded out of my own life. It's on those days that I probably give myself the greatest number of Golden Suns. I give them to myself every fifteen minutes or so until I get out of my funk. There really are no limits to Golden Suns. Once my clients begin doing them regularly, they start noticing more often when they are low on Golden Sun energy; they can quickly respond, giving themselves Golden Suns as often as they like.

Because most people learn through contrast, it's a good idea to experiment with how often you give them. For example, you might choose a day where you fill up with a Golden Sun every hour on the hour. Then, on another day, fill up with just one Golden Sun at the end of the day. This exercise tends to help people gain a better understanding of what their Golden Sun does for them. By experimenting, you will learn when, how, and why to use Golden Suns to best suit your specific needs. Everyone has their own personal relationship with energy. Trust what feels best for you.

Golden Suns can be especially good to do in particular circumstances that help you

Get your personal power back. Golden Suns are very helpful to visualize when you are feeling defeated, vulnerable, or a little spiritually weak.

Represent your unique light. Prolonged use of your Golden Sun will help you become more authentic and heal yourself instantaneously.

Revitalize and restore yourself. Just like when you reset or reboot your electronics, Golden Suns offer you a fresh start and outlook. Often this reboot also feels like a burst of energy and can be great to visualize when you are feeling tired or sluggish.

USING THE GOLDEN SUN TOOL

Now take a moment to close your eyes again and visualize the steps of the Golden Sun tool on your own. This time, try setting an intention after your Golden Sun is full of your gold light.

Step 1: Imagine a bright Golden Sun hovering two feet above your head.

Step 2: Visualize your name in the center of the Golden Sun.

Step 3: Watch as the Golden Sun fills all the way up with gold light, representing all your own energy.

Step 4: Once the Golden Sun is full, set an intention, and then poke a hole in the bottom of it and watch as its liquid fills you up from toe to head.

A couple years ago, Tim started meditating at night before bed. He told himself to start small—to just sit down long enough to give himself a Golden Sun, which took about one minute. He often ended up wanting to spend more time in meditation, visualizing and engaging other energy tools. At other times, he would just focus on his breath or a mantra.

Giving himself a Golden Sun helped Tim develop greater self-awareness, which is the beauty of experiential learning.

One of the first things Tim loved about his Golden Sun wasn't even filling up with it; rather, it was checking in with himself by noticing its position above him—specifically when it was off center, which Tim began to understand usually meant that he was a bit disconnected from his feelings and not prioritizing himself. Tim also noticed his Golden Sun out in front of him, which, according to Daoism, suggests future-oriented thinking and anxiety. But now that Tim has been practicing the Golden Sun Tool for nearly ten years, most often, he tells me, that his suns appear directly above his head. This suggests that he is a lot more comfortable with his power and with being seen for it. He is not surprised that he feels confident, at peace, and on his game.

I know some people also see their Golden Suns behind them, which often represents being stuck in the past or past-oriented thinking. It's like the idea of glory days and usually comes with a limiting belief of "I'll never have it that good again." What's key is just noticing the position of the Golden Sun without judgment; judgment only blinds us from seeing the truth.

Energetic Awareness

The more you practice giving yourself Golden Suns, the more you will become aware of your own energy. For example, you may occasionally notice that your Golden Sun doesn't fill all the way up, or when you poke a hole in it, it doesn't fill you all the way up before you become distracted and lose focus. Others notice air bubbles in their Golden Suns, or sometimes they will only fill in certain parts of themselves with gold light. Whatever the case, it's often reflective of our difficulty to receive, be fully nourished, and valued.

Especially for people like me, who grew up under the impression that children are to be seen and not heard, you may feel like you are going to get in trouble if you fill all the way up with your Golden Sun. As though self-love is selfish or pretentious. It took me a really long time to love myself enough to fill up fully with my Golden Sun. One arm wouldn't fill up, or sometimes, my Golden Sun would fly away from me just after I poked a hole in the bottom of it!

Self-awareness is the pathway to self-mastery.

Before I knew about these tools, I could have sworn that I was confident. But once I was introduced to them, I came to understand that they actually presented a more accurate story than the one I had been telling myself. As I started commanding my Golden Sun directly above my head, I started walking through life with greater certainty. The better I filled up with my own personal power, the better my sleep would be and the less bloated I would feel. Golden Suns simultaneously heal my insecurities and show me where my insecurities remain.

Like everyone, I still have days where my Golden Sun is a little bit off. That said, I'm happy to say it doesn't appear too far out into the future anymore. Yet, sometimes it still bounces around a bit and does not let me fill it up with my personal power. And sometimes I still catch it positioned off to the side and not directly above me. Now, I appreciate the feedback because I know exactly what to do with it.

Case Study

Raul—From Over-Working to Feeling Worthy

Raul had been a peacekeeper his whole life; he began by mediating his parents' fights as a kid. He was conflict averse and just wanted everyone to get along. For example, if coworkers were arguing over strategy, he would step in to offer solutions, which often resulted in him taking on more responsibility. His boss grew to rely on him incessantly but never rewarded Raul's efforts with a raise or a promotion, something Raul asked for only once. Raul was the glue holding everything together, and he knew it, but he felt like Cinderella caught in a hamster's wheel, crowded out of his own life. He knew the office didn't respect him, and he wasn't sure if he respected himself. He didn't know what to do.

Raul began to offer himself Golden Suns with each of his accomplishments any time he felt inclined to say yes, when he was exposed to conflict and whenever he felt uncomfortable about virtually anything. Raul used Golden Suns each time he replied to an email, took care of a task, or did anything he valued. Just because his environment didn't reflect his value back to him didn't mean he had to agree with that sentiment. The Golden Sun "reward system" helped Raul acknowledge himself and better recognize where his energy was leaking.

He quit! Raul realized his worth, followed through with a recruiter, and found a new job that pays more and demands less! The new environment allows him the opportunity to create a new first impression and set boundaries from the start. He's still a peacekeeper, only now he does it consciously. Not all battles are his to mediate, so he is more selective about where he places his energy. He feels respected in his new work setting, especially by himself!

Your Golden Sun, Your Answers

The tools in this book are energy tools, and energy is fluid, so please keep in mind that the position and the appearance of the Golden Sun aren't hard and fast rules. They are more like generalized patterns that resonate with most people. But there are always outliers, unique experiences, and exceptions. Trust that whatever you experience is what is right for you at any given moment in time.

To learn about why your Golden Sun is where it is located, get into the habit of going directly to the source and asking, for example, "Why are you tilted to the right, as opposed to the left?" You can use questions as your own personal divination tool to gain access to your most current answers. Curiosity will keep you fluid with yourself. Remember that change is the only constant. It's also a sign of growth! Being open to whatever your answer may be suggests that you are allowing yourself to grow and not feeling too fixed or stagnant in your identity and self-understanding.

Chinese medicine tends to associate your right side with the masculine (yang), or the giving parts of you, whereas the left tends to reflect the feminine (yin), or the receiving parts of you. Therefore, if your Golden Sun tilts to the right, it's likely you feel more empowered in a position of giving than

receiving. I know this to be true for me. I sometimes pur-
posely place my Golden Sun above my left shoulder for a
couple hours just to help me get more comfortable receiving.
Believe it or not, if I don't reposition it, sometimes it's almost
as though I feel a loss of power when receiving.

Checking in with our Golden Suns is a way of checking
in with ourselves. It can take a while to get the hang of the
dimensions of the Golden Sun, however. We humans are so
used to the tangible material world that it is hard for us to
grasp the dynamism of energy. Energy expands and contracts,
and our energy body is far larger than our human form. The
energy in a house-sized Golden Sun, for example, can easily
consolidate and fill perfectly into the human form. And if
there is overflow, even better! After your body is full, the gold
light can fountain out of your head and into your aura (the
average aura is about four feet in diameter).

Let's not forget that this is *your* source energy that you
are filling up with. It helps you feel and be more like yourself.
You are the authority of you.

If filling up with your source energy feels like a bit too
much, you can bend over and imagine letting some of the
Golden Sun pour out of your head. My teacher would do
that all the time. Because he would get a little too hyper
when he filled up with all of his source energy, he would be
sure to fill in every single cell to avoid any empty pockets
where external energy might be able to land. Once his body
and chakras were full, he would bend forward and let the
rest of his Golden Sun liquid wash over the layers of his
aura to heal them and then allow the gold to evaporate.
That works, too!

I prefer a thick, viscous Golden Sun, and the more viscous
the better! My teacher, on the other hand, preferred an almost
a vapor-like consistency. Your Golden Sun, your preferences!

I often think about the process of developing the habit of embodying Golden Suns as being similar to learning how to have better posture. Imagine you have been slouching your entire life. Slouching would, therefore, feel comfortable to you, right? Even though slouching overdevelops some muscles while keeping others underdeveloped, and even though it perpetuates a lack of balance within, if that's your norm, then it's going to feel predictable, familiar, and comfortable. But let's say that one day you decide to start standing more erect. You know that good posture is said to reduce back pain, but because you have not experienced anatomically correct posture before, at first standing with an erect spine feels uncomfortable. Your underdeveloped muscles are being worked in new ways—possibly for the first time. They may even get sore. Meanwhile, your overdeveloped muscles are not being utilized as much as they are used to and that feels off. Because they have been overdeveloped, they are stronger than your underdeveloped muscles. They are going to want to come in and help out. Standing erect could even feel like you are off balance and something is wrong.

As Golden Suns become your new normal, you will be able to notice when you are leaking or lacking your own personal energy. If you are not being fueled by your Golden Sun, then you are likely being fueled by environmental energy—the energy all around you. In other words, you are being fueled by noise rather than your truth. What used to feel like your comfort zone of disempowerment will start to feel foreign and uncomfortable, while your new comfort zone is you standing in your power.

These tools help honor your personal power, but because honoring your personal power is an underdeveloped muscle, it may feel weird, painful, or foreign at times. As your intuitive mind gets stronger, it will give your rational mind a little break; you will be able to rely on it more and more, and its gifts will only grow.

I remember when I first started keeping a gratitude journal. At first, it was like pulling teeth to find things to be grateful for. That experience quickly transitioned into my being overwhelmed by the abundance of things I had to be grateful for. Before I knew it, I couldn't wait to report back to the journal all the wonderful things that happened to me on a given day. I had gotten into the habit of witnessing my blessings as they were happening and being more mindful of how incredibly blessed I am. The truth is, my life circumstances hadn't changed much from when I first started keeping the gratitude journal, but my mindset had.

The Golden Sun is kind of like that too. Your awareness expands, and you start noticing things from an energetic perspective, not just an analytical one. You will soon start connecting the dots like, *Hmm, I always need like five Golden Suns after talking to that person. If I feel depleted when hanging with them, why do I keep going back for more?*

So, eventually, you will not only rely on your Golden Sun to fill your cup and feel better in the moment, but you will also utilize it as a way to check in with your whole self—your energy self, your consciousness, your sacred gift. You might even set your Golden Sun to this intention: *I observe my Golden Sun to learn about and master myself.*

Case Study

Bru—From Insecurity to Intimacy

Bru was the life of the party! A few drinks in and they would be passing out compliments like candy. Bru was fun, adventurous, and ready for a good time. But, that's the thing: It always took a few drinks. Bru described their social anxiety as crippling. They had never formed intimate friendships on account of it; instead they preferred group settings where there wasn't too much of a spotlight on them, and they could facilitate with liquid courage. This was obviously not a sustainable coping mechanism.

Since Bru associated going out with anxiety, they began a Golden Sun and phone call regimen. They would give themself a Golden Sun before phone dates with friends. Whenever they wanted to reach for a drink, they would fill in with a Sun instead. They got into the habit of giving themself Golden Suns every few minutes when they were being social and every couple of hours when they were not.

Once Bru felt more comfortable with this system, they also felt more comfortable taking their mask off with friends. They felt better going out to dinner with friends instead of constantly meeting up at bars. They grew to trust their impressions of people and realized that sometimes their anxiety was actually their intuition suggesting certain people weren't aligned with them. They still fumble, but overall they are a lot more confident in themself and feel more connected and fulfilled in their friendships.

Your Source Energy

The most common feedback we receive from students and others who use these tools is that this work is like years of therapy in one sitting. That's because the work is rooted in energy, not ego. We go directly to the source to heal, learn, and create. This is different from healing modalities that are anchored in the mind or in the body—therapy and bodywork, for example—which are excellent complements to this work.

In Daoism, the body is a servant to the mind and the mind is a servant to the spirit. Thus, if you change your energy (spirit), it will change your mind, which will change your body. Golden Suns are a reflection of your source energy. Filling up with them will create a ripple effect into your mind and into your life. You will feel more confident, empowered, and present. You will start making decisions from a place of power, rather than from past pain or a place of depletion, inadequacy, or fear. Can you imagine anyone choosing an emotionally unavailable partner from a place of power? We have never seen it.

In the Western world it is such a foreign concept for us to think *energy over matter*; many of us still think, "I'll believe it when I see it." This work, on the other hand, essentially asks us to believe it first in order to see it second. But we also know that thoughts become things in the Western world. We do realize and acknowledge that all that is currently tangible and visible (the matter) was first invisible as it was once merely a thought (the mind).

Yet our world appears to be moving in the direction of acknowledging the presence and even importance of all kinds of things we cannot see. We are already saying things like "mind over matter," and we realize science shows us that everything and anything broken down to its smallest particle is energy in motion. These tools help us connect with that energy in motion and redirect the motion of that energy, if we so choose. In this way, the approach is energy over matter.

One of the most important takeaways about the Golden Sun tool is that it replenishes us with our own source energy, which is the most optimal fuel for our respective bodies.

Sure, your friend's energy fueling your system will work some, but it won't work optimally. Being fueled by our friends or anything else in our environment is like filling up a new car with poor quality gasoline when it requires premium. The subpar gas might work okay for a while, but the car will run more efficiently and last longer when you fuel it with the appropriate gas for its make and model. After practicing and developing a habit with Golden Sun energy, you will feel it when the energy in your space is not your own. Noise in your space can feel like apathy, brain fog, indecision, or even hopelessness. But after a Golden Sun, you will be clearer about who you are and what you want. Our Golden Suns remind us of our alignment and keep us aligned.

＊

I taught Tim how to talk to his Golden Sun—how to literally ask it, "Why are you in front of me today or why are you running away from me today?"—and to take in whatever comes up. Tim often gets the same feedback, but sometimes the response he gets changes. He told me that one time his Golden Sun was tilted off to the side, like at ten o'clock instead of directly above him.

"I figured it was just an indication that I was too tired to get in alignment with my personal power. However, this particular day my Golden Sun told me that I was fully aware of my personal power; I was just hesitant to align with it because of the consequences doing so can bring. I wasn't avoiding my power; I was avoiding my responsibility. It blew my mind! On that particular day, a friend of a friend misidentified me as 'gay' (I identify as queer).

"After checking in with my Golden Sun, I recognized that I didn't feel disempowered by being referred to as gay. Rather, I was avoiding the responsibility of explaining why I identify as queer and not gay, what queer means to me, and so on. I didn't correct them. I just let it be. Had I not checked in with my Golden Sun, I may have actually believed that I wasn't proud of my identity, an outdated belief I once had. At the time, I would often make sure my Golden Sun was just above my head so I was in alignment with my power. I quickly learned, however, that being in alignment with my power and fully embodying and expressing my power are different things."

I reassured Tim that he was getting to know his Golden Sun before he had trusted it to fill him up. Though some people dive right in and Golden Sun themselves up, others, like Tim, take some time to check in with their Golden Sun for days, weeks, or months before actually filling up with it. Filling up with the Golden Sun is the most healing, but knowing where your Golden Sun is located is also a powerful tool in self-understanding.

Losing Personal Energy

Through practice, you will begin to become aware of when Golden Suns serve you best. You will also likely develop greater awareness of how often you lose your personal energy throughout a given day. Please be gentle with yourself. It is completely natural to lose some of your personal energy when you're interacting with others and the material world around you. It is almost impossible not to.

If and when this happens, please acknowledge that it is wonderful that you have developed a personal relationship with an intuitive tool that can help you. These tools exist for a reason—we didn't make them up. Different versions of them have existed for thousands of years across many cultures throughout the world.

As you read this book, recognize that you are interacting with what is written, and therefore, you are exchanging energy with it. You are giving the book some energy and are taking on some of the energy that is embedded in it. In this way, we all are involved in the energetic exchange as we collectively engage in a shared understanding of the material. In this case, the energy exchange serves a greater purpose and is not taxing or depleting.

What is key is learning how to replenish yourself with a Golden Sun the moment you detect energy loss. This way, it is as if you have not lost energy at all. Conserving your energy is great, and different people will lose different amounts of energy, depending on boundaries, habits, and sensitivities; once you get the hang of it, you will see that it is easy to fill back up. Simply fill up when you inevitably lose energy, and trust that you are doing the work.

And always remember:

 Energy follows intention.

The more you give yourself Golden Suns, the more familiar it will feel and the less likely you will be to lose as much energy. Remember, practicing these tools is like building up a muscle. The more you train it, the stronger it becomes and the less energy you need to invest in order to maintain its strength. The more sensitive and empathic a person is, the greater the energy exchange. Let's pick this convo back up in Chapter 3 when we talk about how the Separation tool helps us retain and conserve most of our energy.

Offering Golden Suns

Clients and students ask me whether it is possible to give Golden Suns to others in order to help them. I remember wanting to give Golden Suns to the whole world when I first discovered this energy tool.

Here's a quick lesson in energy ethics. Always ask permission first—either verbally or telepathically—to honor the other person's free will. When asking verbally is an option, simply say, "Hey, would you like me to offer you a Golden Sun? It will call your energy back and help you feel revitalized." You might want to let the recipient know that although you are the one gifting them the Golden Sun, it represents their energy and not yours. In this way, you are not doing something *to* them. You are helping them remember and heal themselves. It's kind of like if someone's money falls out of their pocket and you notice it before they do: "Oh, hey, you dropped this, here you go."

To ask the intended recipient of the Golden Sun permission nonverbally or intuitively, simply offer the question telepathically without any judgment or attachment to the answer. Be sure it's a question, "Would you like a Golden Sun?" and not a demand, "You need a Golden Sun." When neutral and completely unbiased, you will receive the response loud and clear. It is usually an enthusiastic yes, although sometimes there's an adamant no, or an occasional casual shoulder-shrug, "Sure." Trust whatever comes up. And sometimes no answer is the correct answer. In this case no answer means no consent.

It's so important to honor other people's paths and not impose our will on them. When studying addiction and recovery in my doctorate program, one of the first things we learned was about patient desire and its influence on the results of the treatment. When patients come in looking to quit smoking, drinking, overeating, shopping, and the like because their spouse or parent sent them in, the results tend to be temporary at best, regardless of compliance. The patients will do everything "right"—go to all the meetings, the healing sessions, and the support groups; take all the supplements, and so on—and will still relapse. Why? Their soul isn't engaged in the process, so it doesn't fully land. They are simply going through the motions and not connecting with the recovery. They don't actually *want* to quit; what they really want is to please their loved ones.

On the other hand, when patients voluntarily come in and are eager to recover, long-lasting results are far more common. The process is often more gratifying and may involve additional personal breakthroughs and revelations. In other words, when your soul shows up, the work goes deep.

Offering Golden Suns to a willing recipient feels that much more rewarding for you as well. When the recipient is not willing, you may feel invalidated, like your friend just threw away your beautiful gift. I advise following the Golden Rule when offering Golden Suns: If you wouldn't want someone to impose their will onto you, avoid imposing your will onto others.

If we don't honor other people's free will, we are messing with their karma. It prevents them from mastering their own lessons and only distracts us from mastering ours. Stay in your own lane, and you will go much further down your path and at a more accelerated pace. Every time you veer into other people's lanes, you are actually getting farther away from yourself, which doesn't help your ascension or evolution.

Case Study

Anoushka—From Fuming to Fulfilled

To most people, it seemed as if Anoushka had it all. Even Anoushka realized how privileged she was, but she still wasn't happy. She was jealous of just about everyone for everything—their marriages, their homes, their careers, their bodies. Anoushka couldn't help but compare herself to her friends, and each time she did, she fell short. To Anoushka, everyone in the world had it better than she did. She was horribly unfulfilled and could not connect to her many, many blessings.

Anoushka gave herself and all of her possessions Golden Suns. Golden Suns fill us up and help us align with our light, and thereby, they connect us with our purpose. Anoushka was obviously disconnected from source, and no amount of money, experiences, or possessions would feel as satiating as her being fueled by her own bright light. By Golden Sunning all the objects in her life, she was reminded that her life was both an extension and a reflection of her.

Anoushka grew to love her possessions, her life, and her unique aesthetic taste. She learned where her authenticity was and when she was acting out of envy. Over the course of six months, she started choosing friendships, conversations, purchases, and experiences more mindfully. Anoushka allowed her unique personality to shine through more. After months of Golden Suns, rejection wasn't as threatening anymore, so being seen wasn't so risky. The more she was connected to her source energy, the more she felt fulfilled.

Chapter Summary

Your Golden Sun is a tool to help you get your power back. The more you use it, the more you will start becoming aware of what excites you and offers you energy as distinct from what exhausts you and depletes your energy. You will feel more empowered, uplifted, whole, and complete when you deploy your Golden Sun.

There are four main steps to empowering yourself with a Golden Sun:

Step 1: Imagine a bright Golden Sun hovering two feet above your head.

Step 2: Visualize your name in the center of the Golden Sun.

Step 3: Watch as the Golden Sun fills all the way up with gold light, representing all of your own energy.

Step 4: Once it is full, poke a hole in the bottom of the Golden Sun and watch as its liquid fills you up from toe to head.

At first you may want to dedicate a few moments in your regular meditation to visualize your Golden Sun. You may continue to do it this way for years. Or you may feel compelled to try it with your eyes open, while running errands, mid conversation, and regularly throughout the day. Whatever works best for you is what is most important.

If you are one of us who struggles with self-esteem and prioritizing, you will find the Golden Sun especially helpful for self-validating so you don't seek this from external resources. Have fun with it, make it your own, and above all, trust that energy follows intention!

SELF-ASSESSMENT

Ask yourself the following questions. On a scale of 1 to 5:

_____   *How energetic am I feeling right now?* (Where 1 is "Lethargic. I feel like a sloth," and 5 is "I feel refreshed like after a good night's sleep.")

_____   *How empowered am I feeling right now?* (Where 1 is "I feel like my life is not my own," and 5 is "I'm capable of anything. I've got this!")

_____   *How authentic am I feeling right now?* (Where 1 is "I'm confused about who I am and what I want," and 5 is "I feel aligned with my true purpose.")

_____   *How present am I feeling right now?* (Where 1 is "I'm not sure how it's possible, but I'm both future tripping and dwelling on the past at the same time," and 5 is "This moment is all I've got. I'm right here right now.")

2

Recognizing Your Energy as Your Own: Grounding Cord Tool

In the circle of fate
We are the dot
Where the compass
Meets the paper.
—HAFIZ

Releasing Energy

Let's face it, if you are reading this, you are a person who feels things deeply. It's also likely that people in your orbit feel supported by you. This is beautiful! Please honor it. As Anita Moorjani says, "sensitive is the new strong." Let's work with your strengths by taking a moment to reflect on how feeling things deeply impacts your daily life.

- When you interact and connect with others, how do you feel when you part ways, or when the conversation is over? Do you sometimes feel as if you are carrying their experience with you?

- Have you ever noticed yourself replaying the same conversation over and over again in your head?

- Do you sometimes get tired of feeling it all, all the time?

First of all, know that taking on other people's energy is an inevitable part of the human experience. When this happens, we can feel out of sorts, depleted, or overly concerned about someone else's situation. What is key is recognizing when what you are feeling doesn't belong to you, and then releasing the noise the moment you realize that's what's influencing you. Wouldn't it be nice to have a step-by-step guide to shake it off when life is irking you?

Rest assured; the Grounding Cord tool is at your service! In this chapter, you are introduced to this tool, which will help you release after connecting with others. This chapter helps you recognize your energy, distinguish your energy from others', and release unwanted energy from your space. By visualizing, you will get out of your head and back into your power.

GROUNDING CORD AS MEDICINE	GROUNDING CORD AS RITUAL
When you are overwhelmed with emotion and want to declutter your head to think clearly	Before important conversations or events
When the way you are feeling is not serving you	After an exchange with someone
During moments of chaos or unwanted intensity	When you go to the bathroom (I mean, if you are already releasing physically, why not do it energetically, as well?)
When you find yourself being overly reactive	Each time you wash your hands
When you realize you are prioritizing others above yourself	When you take out the trash
When you can't help yourself from overthinking	Before falling asleep

In just a moment, you will be guided through the steps for the Grounding Cord tool. Before you begin, take a moment to assess how you are feeling right now.

Visualizing

In a moment, you will allow your eyes to close and look within. Start slowing down your breath to begin box breathing as described here.

Inhale for four counts, then hold your breath for four counts, then exhale for four counts, and then hold for four counts. Repeat. Inhale for 4, 3, 2, 1; hold for 4, 3, 2, 1; exhale for 4, 3, 2, 1; hold for 4, 3, 2, 1.

You will focus your energy, attention, and awareness on your hips. Imagine that you are sitting above the center of a hollow tube that is about two feet in diameter; the tube extends from your hips all the way down and into the center of the Earth. This is your grounding cord. Whether you imagine it beneath you while you're sitting upright or lying down, your grounding cord is your energetic vehicle that you will use to let go of

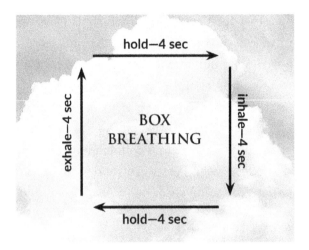

unwanted energies in your body and energy field. Just visualize your grounding cord as a tube that is below you and still energetically connected to you. It is going straight down, right through any materials that may be there—your seat or bed, the floor, another apartment perhaps—until it reaches the core of Earth and you see, feel, or experience it anchored into the center of the Earth.

If you haven't already done so, please take a moment to close your eyes and try visualizing this for yourself.

Wonderful! How was that?

Welcome to your Grounding Cord tool! Please trust that whatever experience you just had was the right experience for you, even if you are not sure if you visualized it or not. These tools grow more potent and powerful with each use. This also means that it will get gradually easier to visualize, utilize, trust, and rely on them. You are well on your way to commanding the energy of your day! In a couple moments, you will be prompted to close your eyes again and visualize additional details of your grounding cord.

Your Release, Your Cord

Your grounding cord is uniquely yours and is made out of any material you desire. It is custom made, just for you, for this exact moment in time. It could be made of metal, glass, or crystals; it could even be a hollowed-out tree trunk that you are sitting on top of. Whatever material you choose today is the right material for you today. Trust whatever comes to you.

You also will notice that your grounding cord is consistent all the way through from your hips down into the center of the Earth without any holes, tears, or gaps in it. Should you see anything that needs mending or repair, simply imagine that repair happening, like the holes closing in effortlessly. Whether you are seeing it and are confident in this or not, please trust that the energy is doing what you are commanding it to do.

Now take a moment to close your eyes and imagine your unique grounding cord.

Yay! How did that go?

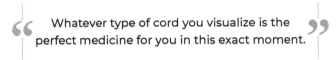

> **Whatever type of cord you visualize is the perfect medicine for you in this exact moment.**

Eventually, you will begin to feel a gravitational pull each time you ground with your Grounding Cord tool. For some people, using the Grounding Cord tool feels like taking a deep sigh or being overcome with a sense of calm. You might feel your body getting heavier and heavier as you release unwanted energies down into the center of the Earth. Once you have released them, you will feel lighter, brighter, more focused, and trusting that the universe has your back.

When I think about the grounding cord, I am often reminded of the fact that energy is neither created nor destroyed. When you imagine releasing through your grounding cord, you are imagining giving energy back to the Earth. The Earth neutralizes it and repurposes it. The Earth is here to support us; it just needs our trust to do its work.

We also can't help but think about gravity when we engage our grounding cord. Because gravity is a force of nature that attracts matter toward the center of the Earth, by virtue of living on this planet, we are all subject to the law of gravity, right? Just like Newton discovered that gravity is responsible for an apple falling down from a tree (rather than falling up or being suspended in air), you can imagine that gravity is also responsible for pulling unwanted energies from your space down into the center of the Earth. When gravity runs through the hollow tube that is your grounding cord, it creates a vacuum. In this way, you can allow gravity to help you release unwanted energies with grace and ease. Just allow gravity to do its thing.

When I first started using my grounding cord, I would occasionally see myself falling down it. Though this is not ideal, it is very common for beginners, and it can occasionally happen even after much practice. Bottom line: This is normal and you are right on track. You can visualize yourself pulling yourself out of your grounding cord as soon as you suspect that you have gone down it. With practice, trust that you will eventually stop falling down your grounding cord.

In a few moments, you will learn how to assign color to unwanted energies in your space and how to send them down your grounding cord. The more you practice watching the colors go down your cord without going down with them, the easier it gets. As with this entire book, practice makes permanent.

Noticing

Some days you will want a wide grounding cord and others you will want it to be narrow. Take note of what feels best and when.

With each new grounding cord, check in with what you need. Do you need to turn the vacuum up a little higher? Do the walls need to be thicker? What material is best for your grounding cord at this specific moment?

Over time most students say they default to a few different grounding cord options. For example, I mostly enjoy a waterfall, but when I'm feeling especially scattered, my go-to grounding cord is made of copper and the walls are extra thick. Tim's grounding cord used to be made of steel, but now it is almost always made of thick glass or a translucent stone like quartz. As you grow and change, the grounding cord that best serves you may grow and change with you.

Another valuable thing to look out for is moments and situations in your daily life in which you feel naturally grounded compared to those where you feel less grounded. We tend to ground when we are out in the forest or surrounded by trees. We mimic them. Similarly, when we are in the company of grounded people we tend to match their energy; the same goes for when we are around less grounded people. Noticing our groundedness in different contexts and situations can be helpful feedback regarding how to best prepare yourself for that time.

Energy Follows Intention

When we say, "energy follows intention," we want you to trust that if you are having any difficulty visualizing, it will get easier and easier with time. It is like building muscle. When you do your first pushup in a long while, it may be challenging to find the appropriate muscles, and it is likely that you will be working some non-pushup muscles at first. With time and practice, however, you can do many pushups without losing form; your body knows which muscles to engage and which muscles not to engage. It gets easier, as does visualizing your grounding cord. First it may appear like a shadow, an outline, or a silhouette of a grounding cord. Some people don't even see their grounding cord at first, but they may feel it or simply acknowledge it. It will all come with time. You are doing the work even if you are not seeing the work. This is an instance of you learning about and healing yourself.

   Energy flows where intention goes.

Case Study

Mia—From Confusion to Clarity

Mia was experiencing overwhelm and confusion. "I don't even know why I'm crying! I'm just so overwhelmed, but I don't even know why!" Mia was a yoga instructor who saw many private clients intimately each day and was perpetually in a new relationship. She had become dependent on external validation. Everyone in Mia's life loved her and looked up to her. She, unfortunately, didn't feel the same about herself.

As a trauma response from being neglected as a child, Mia would unconsciously create a little home within her energetic space for anyone who showed interest in her. She loved carrying around other people's energies because, to her, it felt like love. Mia was an unskilled intuitive, so while she was housing the energy of others within her space, she was also unintentionally feeling all their thoughts and feelings. You can imagine how overwhelming that would be! Pretty much everyone Mia had ever met in her life lived in her body. She was hesitant to let go of them because she was afraid that she would go back to feeling neglected, abandoned, and isolated. She had poor boundaries, but she liked them that way because it made her feel loved and desired.

Mia began visualizing her grounding cord and sending her new partner's energy all the way down it into the center of the Earth, which she did with much reluctance. She did the same with each of the clients she had worked with that day, the previous day, two days prior, and so on. Eventually, she grounded out the energy of everyone she had seen that week and the week before, whether professionally or personally.

Mia was able to stop crying and worrying. The fears left her. The overwhelm left her. Mia was now operating from her own Golden Sun source energy rather than the energy of others.

Grounding cords can offer tremendous peace, calm, and trust. For Mia, the outcome was healthier relationships, yielding greater self-confidence and far less noise within. She learned the difference between what was her energy and what wasn't. She now feels very capable of navigating all that is hers, which has increased her trust in herself and her clarity in her feelings.

Red

Shall we test out your fancy, new grounding cord by sending some energy down it? Let me explain what to pay attention to before you close your eyes and try it out yourself.

First, you will imagine your body with the grounding cord below you. Then, you will assign the color red to any energy within your space that is not serving you. The red energy could appear in your feet, your torso, your right ear, your entire body, or even slightly outside of your body, in your *aura*—your energy field.

Next, you will scan your space for the red energy. Just trust the first thing you see or that comes to mind. Where do you see red in your space? Is it in your hands, your head, your legs, your aura? Before you turn your focus onto your grounding cord, see if you can work your intuition muscle and spot the red in your space. Trust whatever it is you are visualizing, experiencing, or intuitively knowing. Take note of where the red is located as a way of cultivating self-awareness.

Now take a moment to close your eyes and try it out for yourself.

Yay! How did that go?

Remember, whatever red you observed or didn't observe in your space is just fine.

You will be sending plenty more red down your grounding cord over time, so the more you start to perceive it in your space, the more you will be able to observe whether it appears in the same locations, is the same shade of red, or if it changes each time you engage your grounding cord. Start collecting feedback and data to better understand yourself and your patterns. The more you become familiar with your energy, the more you will be able to distinguish what is not yours. The more you release what is not you, the more authentic you become. Intuitive awareness and authenticity go hand in hand.

In a moment, you will close your eyes again and visualize the red going down your grounding cord. Wherever the red is, and whether you see it or not, you will command that it move toward your grounding cord.

Because your grounding cord acts as a vacuum, the moment the red is near your hips or lower back, it gets sucked all the way down your grounding cord until it disappears into the Earth. You will watch, feel, or experience all the red leaving your space, entering your grounding cord, and easily and effortlessly moving all the way down your cord until it gets absorbed by the Earth.

Once the unwanted energy is absorbed by the Earth, the Earth will neutralize it and redistribute it back into the world, where our planet will make better use of it. Everyone wins.

Now give it a try. Close your eyes and visualize the red in your space going down your grounding cord.

How was that?

> " Please keep in mind that one of the major benefits of this book is to learn how to control energy. You do not have to sit back and let energy control you! "

Please continue with the visualization even if you are not seeing the red in your space. Go through the motions, build those energy pathways, work your intuition muscle, and your command of energy will grow stronger—it's inevitable. Keep at it. Just like we crawl before we walk, you may be slowly exploring these energy tools at first. Your insight will transition from foggy and vague to vivid and illuminating as you grow and learn to master these tools.

USING THE GROUNDING CORD TOOL

Now take a moment to close your eyes and try to visualize the steps of the Grounding Cord tool on your own.

Step 1: Imagine a hollow tube around your hips that connects you to the Earth's center.

Step 2: Scan your energy field for colors or energies to send down your grounding cord that are charged and competing with your authenticity.

Step 3: Command, watch, feel, or trust that the colors, energies, and sensations are being sucked down your grounding cord where they are absorbed into the center of the Earth.

Blue

Give it another go by closing your eyes, envisioning your grounding cord, and releasing the color blue. Feel free to stop and close your eyes whenever you like from now through the remainder of the chapter.

Scan your space for the color blue. Where is the blue? Take a moment to tune into how you feel when you are vibrating at blue. Just observe and take note before you let go.

How does it feel? Do you see or perceive the blue in one particular area? Multiple areas? Nowhere at all? Simply observe and accept whatever comes through.

Next, send all the blue energy down your grounding cord. Remember, if you are having trouble seeing the blue, that's okay! You are doing the work. Just trust that you are commanding the blue.

Once your blue starts to make its way toward your hips, your grounding cord sucks it down and out of your space. Watch, feel, or simply intend that the blue leaves your space and travels down your grounding cord, making its way from the top of your grounding cord all the way down until it disappears into the center of the Earth. You may see the blue floating down your grounding cord, or dancing as it moves like smoke or food coloring in a tube of water. Or maybe you see the blue going down your grounding cord shaped like little blue balls, zipping down quickly as if being sucked by a vacuum. Whatever you experience is just right for you.

Please now take a brief moment to acknowledge the absence of blue. You are no longer able to see, feel, or function from the color blue.

Scan yourself once more. How does the absence of blue from your space feel?

The more we release energy that competes with our power, the more we make space for our personal power, our own gold light. As we do this, we start to feel more like ourselves.

Before we continue, let's talk a little bit about releasing energy that is not of service to you. Let's call this *charged energy*. When you release it back to the Earth, it becomes uncharged and returns to its neutral state.

You will remember that with the Golden Sun tool your own energy is the energy that works best for you. In this way, your Golden Sun energy has no charge. When you are vibrating off of your own personal gold light, you are feeling in your power, you are confident and enthusiastic about life. Use your Golden Sun to keep connected to your personal power. Use your grounding cord to release charged energy—anything that is not your own gold light.

All feelings, emotions, and thoughts possess a charge. Think about when you are angry; you are likely wanting a specific outcome, right? You may want to feel heard and for your perspective to be validated, or you may want justice to be served or for someone to admit fault or be reprimanded for their actions. A common belief with charged feelings or thoughts is "but it shouldn't be like this."

Neutral energy, on the other hand, suggests no desires or attachments to outcome. When we feel neutral energy, we are able to accept things exactly as they are.

Later in this book, you will learn about the Center of Your Head tool, which will help you perceive energy from a neutral perspective. As Tim mentioned before, this process is similar to how anthropologists approach studying other cultures: As an anthropologist, Tim's job is to learn about another culture from the inside out, not to arrive at the culture with his own agenda in place for how the people he is studying should act or what they should believe. When he checks his ego when conducting fieldwork, he is able to take in whatever information arises during his observations more freely. The same goes when you look at energy from a neutral position. There's no need to judge. Be gentle and just observe to understand. Do your best to see like an anthropologist.

Ultimately, it's important to remember that charged energy is everywhere as it helps us make sense of the world. It is a construct of the human experience that takes shape through language, culture, and society. It is not an effect of energy; it is an effect of our minds, our collective, and our shared common understandings of values assigned to experiences.

Let's continue releasing colors.

Purple

Next, release the color purple. This time, assign value to the purple. You can assign confusion, uncertainty, doubt, or insecurity energy to this color. This way, when you release the purple, you will be releasing this energy. Scan your body and energy field for the color purple. Trust whatever you are receiving or seeing. This is feedback for you and will help you better understand yourself. As you continue to do the work, start looking for energy patterns that may present themselves. Take note if the purple is always in the same place, if it moves around, or how it feels to let go of it relative to other colors.

Regardless of whatever you are seeing, feeling, or receiving, you are able to heal yourself and release the purple by focusing on moving it down your grounding cord. Watch as the purple goes all the way down your cord, working with the law of gravity so the process is easy and effortless, moving all the way down until the Earth absorbs it completely. The purple is completely gone. Check back in with yourself and acknowledge how you feel after releasing the purple. Chances are you are feeling a bit lighter, more inspired and confident. Committing this sensation to memory will help reinforce this work and help you ground passively so that you can simply create a grounding cord every day and trust it to release charged energy throughout the day as it comes up.

Green

You tend to carry the energy of those you love and admire the most and those that irritate you the most. You are likely carrying the energy of whomever first comes to mind, so release it now. Imagine that this person's energy is the color green in your space. Scan your space for the color green. Are you carrying their green energy in your hands, feet, heart, head, back, or shoulders?

Now send the green down your grounding cord. You can do this whether you are certain of the green or not. Simply imagine the green near your back and hips and watch as it goes all the way down from your hips until it disappears into the center of the Earth. As mentioned earlier, the Earth neutralizes and redistributes this energy. In this case, it is neutralizing this green energy and sending it back to the person from whom it originated. Imagine that person receiving this energy with a smile on their face; they get a little more aligned, happier, and healthier as they receive their energy. Meanwhile, you have just made more space for your own gold light energy so you can be the best version of yourself.

You may use your grounding cord to release charged conversations, feelings, moments, or experiences. Whatever it is, simply give it a color and send that color down your grounding cord.

Case Study

Jade—From Giving to Grounding

It was easy to love Jade because they would always reflect the best parts of those in their orbit and often had something encouraging to say. They were so sweet.

Jade was the type of person who delighted in helping others and went out of their way to accommodate them. They knew everyone's favorite restaurants and dishes, so when they and their friends were deciding where to meet up or what to eat, Jade often suggested whatever their friends loved instead of what Jade loved. It didn't even occur to them that they might desire something different!

Their calendar was always packed with commitments, and they would regularly say yes to invitations without even taking into consideration whether they wanted to attend or not. Unsurprisingly, Jade felt stretched thin, yet they simultaneously loved their community and their life so much that they were hesitant to cut out any people or events. In fact, Jade had no room for Jade in Jade's space or life.

Does this sound familiar? It's a pretty common pattern among empaths. Jade was over-giving at an unsustainable pace while they were telling and convincing themselves that they were deeply fulfilled and grateful to have so many friends.

Jade began the process of grounding out people. They grounded out the energy of their coworkers, friends, family, and the person they were dating. Their eyes suddenly went from looking dull and somewhat exhausted to clear and vibrant.

Their perspective shifted too! They began seeing with more clarity and no longer scheduled events for the week ahead. Pleasantly surprised by their newfound clarity, the only commitment Jade made for the following week was to their grounding cord. They put themself on a regimen of grounding for ten minutes three times daily. Three times each day, various colors representing the many people in Jade's life and energy field would swirl right down Jade's grounding cord and disappear into the Earth. Jade would then visualize the people these colors belonged to growing three sizes when they got their energy back, as though it was some sort of video game. Jade got more creative with grounding and started to have more fun with it.

Jade found the clarity in their preferences, needs, and desires to be profound. Their schedule started to reflect their priorities. They started to have an easy time letting people and experiences go. They felt a sense of freedom they hadn't known before.

Without all that noise in their space, Jade was able to really listen to their own personal truth and allow that to be their guide. Their interests changed, their relationships elevated, and they became more expressive, opinionated, and enthusiastic about life. For the first time ever, they fell in love with themselves and watched as their self-respect grew over the course of seven months of practicing with their Grounding Cord tool. Go, Jade!

Grounding Cord as a Slide for Others

Inevitably, a handful of students always struggle with the thought of releasing others from their space. We hear statements like these all the time: "I feel bad, like I'm rejecting them or abandoning them," or "What if I really love them and enjoy them in my space?" We get it; it's an adjustment, and it's a concept that may feel like tough love or a little cold or unkind at first.

What I have noticed is that when I don't have my loved ones in my energy field, I actually enjoy my time with them more. For example, my brother really stresses out over timeliness. Because I am his older sister, it pains me to see the way he struggles with things like time management and coordinating time with others. He is consistently ten minutes early and just about everyone in his life tends to run about ten minutes late. The amount of anguish this causes him is a very predictable, recurring pattern, and it is something I can't relate to.

Before being introduced to the Grounding Cord tool, I would rush to meet up with him on time, and more often than not, something would happen that would delay me. Unknowingly, I was running his energy through my field, which caused me to get super anxious over something as simple as a coffee date. I would lose my keys, forget my wallet at home and have to turn back around to get it, and so on. I was not grounded. I was not calm. I was not being myself. I was running his energy in my space and believing his truth was mine. I would show up late and be so remorseful and apologetic. We would energetically both agree that I ruined the coffee date and so the event would follow that tone. I would feel bad and inadequate. We would both feel like he deserved better and that he respected me more than I respected him. We would feel disconnected when by coming together all we wanted was to connect.

When I first started grounding him out, I felt guilty, as though I was dismissing his experience or silencing him. But something happened. Without all of his nervous energy in my field, I started showing up on time! When I'm grounded, I don't lose keys or forget my wallet. When I'm not running his energy in my field, I'm not buying into his truth.

I went from fearing that I would disappoint him to laughing at him and with him about his timeliness. I went from believing I was ruining our time together to pointing out that he's just setting himself up for repeated disappointment when he expects others to be as time-sensitive as he is. This is my truth on the matter and a truth I wasn't able to access with his energy all up in my space. Without him in there, I could see him more clearly on our coffee dates and better connect with him as his sister, rather than just project my resentment all over him. My patience for his timeliness grew, and my time-management improved. Grounding him out of my space didn't disconnect us; it improved our connection and our relationship!

✳

Here's what helped me ground others out without the guilt: a slide to ride! When it is time to ground people out, I turn my grounding cord into a slide. Sometimes it's a waterslide, sometimes it's more of a rollercoaster ride. Either way, the person that I'm grounding out is having fun! I imagine a mini version of that person, rather than assigning them a color. Their miniature goes down the slide with their arms up and exclaims, "weeeee!" Once they reach the center of the Earth, I imagine them turning into liquid gold and filling in their own Golden Sun. This spin on the grounding cord has created a positive association with grounding people out and is a lot of fun to visualize. Explore using a slide or ride for yourself!

Pink

The dimensions and materials of your grounding cord may change from day to day as you are also constantly changing.

Take a moment right now to discover the energy of your grounding cord. Expand the width of your cord until it is about three feet in diameter. Experiment with how that feels for you by sending some pink down your expanded cord. Take this a step further and expand your grounding cord to four feet in diameter. Send some more pink down. Was it easier or more challenging to do this with your grounding cord at this larger size?

Expand your grounding cord a bit more to be about five feet in diameter. What is it like to send pink energy down now? Sometimes a larger grounding cord feels like greater support, whereas at other times it will feel a little overwhelming and less supportive. Your preferences may change depending on situations or events, so do check in regularly. Similarly, you may want to change the material your grounding cord is made of from time to time depending on what the situation calls for.

Adjust your grounding cord to a diameter that feels comfortable to you as you continue to release unwanted energies. Grounding cords often elicit a feeling of safety, security, peace, and calm. Adjust yours until it offers you such feelings.

 Intuitive awareness and authenticity go hand in hand.

Case Study

Cameron—From Healing Unconsciously to Consciously Healing

Cameron was a lovebug with a huge heart who spent time and energy unconsciously healing others. She loved big and hard. She would speak to people's light and not their darkness. Naturally, they would light up in her presence and display the best version of themselves without even meaning to. Cameron brought out the best in people.

Generally speaking, healers tend to attract people who need healing, and many of us are healers without even knowing it. Cameron was a receptionist and would not have considered herself a healer. What she did know is that she would find herself in one relationship after another with people who ultimately drained her of all her energy.

But her relationships didn't always start out that way. Indeed, she would see something in people that they didn't see in themselves, and they would live up to their pure potential for a while. Ultimately, however, the honeymoon period would wear off, and she would start feeling sorry for the people she was dating. They would go from being enthusiastic about life (and her) to revealing how insecure and unworthy they truly felt. Whether they were complaining about work problems, venting about their self-perceived inadequacies, or blaming their parents for many of their adult problems, their shadow sides would eventually peek through.

Cameron couldn't stand to see someone she loved suffer so much or think so little of themselves. As a natural-born healer, she would unknowingly start grounding out their pain and sadness through her own grounding cord. Her spirit was strong and courageous, and deep down she trusted life.

Cameron was naturally grounded, even before she learned of her grounding cord. But she didn't realize she was offering her grounding cord to just about anyone and everyone. At the earliest and slightest hint of discomfort, Cameron's grounding cord would suck all of that color down to the Earth's center. It was as if her energy was saying, "I got this. I can see you are not in a position to help yourself right now, but this is easy for me, so how about I ground that pain out for you?" Cameron was not aware of all of this work; all she knew is that she would start to feel exhausted after a date.

As more time elapsed in her relationships, the imbalance would become more pronounced. Her partners almost started expecting her to ground out their pain. It's like they regressed and became more emotionally immature with time. Whether she realized it or not, she was contributing to this imbalance as it highlighted her strength and sometimes felt affirming. It was almost as though she needed to be needed in this way.

After a while, Cameron learned how to teach others to ground. Up to this point, all Cameron wanted to do was help, but she realized she wasn't actually helping. She learned that working with her strengths and teaching others how to use their own personal grounding cords would be more empowering for these individuals, far healthier for Cameron, and the most sustainable practice for all.

As people came to her for advice, rather than dispensing it or grounding out their pain for them, she would ask, "Are you open to me guiding you in an energy tool that I think could help you out?" Most people said, "Yes! Please!" They were so grateful for her support and guidance. At work, they even asked her to lead a weekly meditation, which she loved. She was being recognized for her healing talents! Yes, a few folks did not want to learn how to ground. They just wanted to talk, vent, complain, and connect with Cameron the way they always had; for Cameron, that was good feedback, too! She started making more time for the folks who would ground for themselves and less time for those who would not.

Cameron is now consciously healing. Although Cameron's grounding of her partners was rooted in compassion, doing the energy work for them actually disempowered them. She began to realize that by grounding out their pain for them, she was suggesting that they were unable to do it for themselves. This is what Pema Chödrön refers to as *idiot compassion* in her book, *The Places That Scare You*. Doing other people's energy work for them enables their pain; it doesn't reduce or dissolve it. It is their pain, so they are the only ones who can heal it. Anyone else attempting to heal them is robbing them of their karmic lessons.

Furthermore, doing so creates much confusion and chaos for both the healer and the relationship. When Cameron was channeling other people's pain and energy in her body, she was squeezing herself out of her own space. The more she did this, the more she confused their experience for her own. Rather than lifting them to higher ground, she ended up sinking to their lows. Thankfully Cameron turned this around. She went from unconsciously healing others at a cost to her own well-being to consciously guiding others in healing themselves.

When I was teaching one of my friends about the Grounding Cord tool, he became a little confused about what we mean when we say you have "unwanted energies in your space." In general, when we refer to *your space*, we are referring to both your body and your energy field, also known as your aura.

As you are grounding energy out of your space, we invite you to imagine that color leaving from both your body and the energy field/aura that surrounds your body. Similarly, as you are calling energy in through your Golden Sun, the invitation is to first fill in your body and then allow the overflow of gold light to fill in your aura so you become a glowing orb of gold light.

 Remember, visualizations will get easier with practice and over time.

By prompting yourself to visualize unwanted energies in your space—red, blue, green, pink; whatever color you assign to them—you become more aware of yourself and your intuition. This energy awareness helps you begin to control and navigate energy rather than letting it control you.

The more aware we are of ourselves, the more aware we are of what is not us, what does not serve us, and what is just taking up space. Other people's energy in our space can be confusing because it can look, act, and feel like our own energy. This is what interferes with our intuition. Being self-aware helps us better understand when this is happening. The second you notice this is happening, take a moment to release that energy and see if you experience more mental clarity. Without all those other cooks in your metaphysical kitchen, this is likely to occur.

Seeing colors other than the one that we are asking you to scan for is your intuition calling out at you, which is wonderful! If we ask you to release all the red and you are also seeing blues and greens, please release those, too! Be proud of yourself for spotting what energy is not yours. You are already tuning into your intuition—please listen to it and trust it!

Gray

Now practice releasing one final color from your space and consciousness. Imagine the color gray, which represents any pain or fear energy in your body or energy field; look for the color gray all over. Take note of where it resides and how it feels when you connect with it. Remember, you are an expert at releasing energy now!

Command all that gray toward your grounding cord, and watch, feel, or experience it going all the way down your cord, flowing down with gravity, until it disappears completely into the center of the Earth so that you no longer see it, feel it, or function from it. Wonderful work!

Be aware that when you use your grounding cord, it will accumulate energy, which will reduce its efficacy. Just like changing out the bag to a vacuum cleaner, it is a good idea to change out your grounding cords for maximum efficacy.

To start, destroy, or release your current grounding cord; simply watch it retract back into the center of the Earth so that it disappears completely. You may take a moment to check in with yourself and this sensation. Do you notice a difference between how it feels to be ungrounded and how it feels to be grounded?

Create a new grounding cord for yourself by imagining a hollow tube made out of a material of your choice that extends from you down into the center of the Earth. Remember that you are sitting on top of this hollow tube and that the force of gravity is running through it. You are welcome to use the same material for this grounding cord as you did for the last one. If you loved the tree trunk you were working with, you are welcome to create a new hollowed-out tree trunk to sit on top of. Be certain that your grounding cord extends all the way into the center of the Earth and that it's directly beneath you and does not veer off in any one direction. Scan your grounding cord now and adjust, mend, or modify it as needed. Great work!

Fill Back Up

After letting go of so much energy, it is wise to consciously fill back in with a Golden Sun. Otherwise, there is a tendency to unconsciously fill in with environmental energy—like the unwanted energies in your space that you just removed! Take a moment to visualize a Golden Sun above you that is filling up with your own bright golden light, and then poke a hole in the bottom of it so it pours into your body and fills you up from toe to head, calibrating you to your authentic self and preventing you from taking on energy that is not yours.

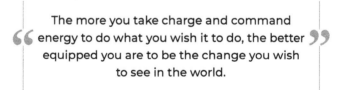

> **The more you take charge and command energy to do what you wish it to do, the better equipped you are to be the change you wish to see in the world.**

Most people who are drawn to this book will likely have some idea of their untapped potential and what powerful energetic beings they are. Some of you may feel disempowered by all you feel and sense in the world—almost as if your intuition is a curse and not a gift. Others of you may simply not know what to do with your untapped potential. You might be hyperaware of problems but do not know what to do about them. You might be thinking, *Great, so I see purple in my space. Now what? How does stating the obvious help me live my best life?*

Identifying colors in your space helps you learn that you can control your energy, and therefore your life. You are not only learning how to tap into your authenticity here, you are also learning how to heal your life and live your best life moving forward.

We are energy in motion. We are all in a constant exchange with the energies in our lives and environments. The more you take charge and command energy to do what you wish it to do, the better equipped you are to be the change you wish to see. Commanding energy gives you your power back. Naturally, the more you exercise this power, the more powerful you will feel, and before you know it, you will be able to visualize your dreams into reality.

Case Study

Jamal—From Absorbing to Emitting

Jamal was easily influenced by environmental energies. He had a hard time with his grounding cord. Sometimes it would hop around. Other times it was too short and wouldn't reach down into the ground. When he could get it to go directly underneath him, without any tears, holes, gaps, jumps, spirals, or shenanigans, he would go right down with it along with the colors! It felt more like his grounding cord had control over him rather than the other way around.

This is a common experience, especially for highly sensitive people. Folks like Jamal have been conduits for energy for most of their lives without even knowing it. It has become almost second-nature for them to absorb and reflect environmental energy. They are so connected to energy outside of themselves that they lose dominance in their own space. The outside world becomes their inside world. Like we say, practice makes permanent. Jamal's lack of command over his own energy field had become a habit.

When your grounding cord goes rogue, it is likely that you are resisting the process. You may find greater comfort in creating and filling than releasing and letting go.

Jamal started with his Golden Sun each time he wanted to ground. He would give himself three Golden Suns before he extended a grounding cord. He loved his Golden Suns! He had such a fun time filling himself up with gold light, and the energizing effects of the Golden Sun were more his vibe than the soothing effects of the grounding cord.

The Golden Suns were like his warm-up visualizations so that when it came time to envision his grounding cord, he was able to apply that muscle and momentum to it. To reinforce a positive relationship with his new tools, I instructed Jamal to only ground for as long as it felt good. If that meant just one minute, then that was perfect. Over time, he began to extend the time he spent grounding little by little, but he continued to fill up with three Golden Suns before he began the process. For him, the Golden Suns were key to grounding. If he felt resistance come up while he was grounding, he could switch back to filling in with a few Golden Suns before he continued to send colors down his grounding cord.

Jamal became the commander of his own vessel. He went from being an energy sponge to shining like a lighthouse. Now his inside world shines through to the outside. Jamal went from losing himself in relationships and feeling out of control in his life to being the creator of his life. In hindsight he realized how easily he was influenced by others. Now, he's more decisive and his actions reflect his authenticity, beliefs, and values. He loves his grounding cord now and has immediate access to it and complete command over it.

Getting Familiar with Grounding

For most, grounding out unwanted energy may feel boring or lonely at first. If you are used to hosting five to ten people in your one-bedroom apartment, and then all of a sudden you are left with just you, it will be an adjustment. You may experience a little bit of a "love hangover" and feel somewhat empty inside once you have released energy that is not yours. Even if you have been working on kicking out the unwanted house guests for years, getting used to them being gone takes some work. And, of course, you may find you have some house guests you don't exactly *want* to kick out, but you know doing so is a healthy thing to offer your relationship.

Personally, I had a hard time letting go of my anger. She was almost like a friend, and I loved her! My anger gave me personality, passion, spice, *and* she left me exhausted and out of integrity. I had overly identified with my anger and wasn't sure who I would be without her. Letting her go felt almost like an identity crisis. Would I be another boring pushover without all this anger? I was obviously attached to my anger, which made her more challenging to release.

Welp! I did it! I grew a healthy relationship with my grounding cord and started leaning on it more regularly. I found out that being grounded is neither boring, nor empty, nor lonely!

Once you get used to being grounded, you recognize it as peaceful, soothing, and expansive. If it doesn't seem that way right now, it's just because it's a foreign feeling that you are still getting used to. You are doing your best to make sense of it and maybe the closest experience that you have had to this is boredom or loneliness. In my case, I hadn't grown up with peaceful role models, so it took me a while to recognize what I was feeling was *peace*—not apathy, indifference, boredom, or anything else I had experienced in the past. It was a new feeling for me and one I had to adjust to.

Once you get grounded, it's kind of like the point of no return. Once I adjusted to the peace, my tolerance for chaos was much lower. It took me years to get here. If you are more naturally grounded than me, it may just take you a few months or weeks, or maybe even days!

It can take some time for your Grounding Cord tool or any of these energy tools to become your go-to tools, allies, guides, or healing modalities. You will likely find your-self falling back into the old habit of hosting a wide array of charged energy in your field in your pursuit of getting grounded. This is common and a natural part of the learning curve. While you are building this new muscle, you are also simultaneously neglecting some old muscles. It's *a lot*. You are both creating new neural pathways and resisting the old, comfy ones, all at the same time. You rock! Focus on *progress* not *perfection*.

We are creatures of habit, after all, which is why it's imperative that you continue to practice these tools, even when you are not feeling them or are not perceiving results. Build the habit, and the habit will hold you when you need it most. After you have tasted being grounded, hosting as many people in your space will feel different. It likely won't feel like love or a slumber party anymore. What once felt like applause and cheers might just feel like noise and interference, chaos, or confusion. The best feeling is when you recognize this newer sensation for what it is: peace and clarity.

Ultimately, you will get to a place where you can literally throw a party and host many people in your one-bedroom home and still feel like you are the only person living there. That is to say, you will be better equipped to juggle many balls, be as social as you wish to be, or throw yourself into new adventures. It's like switching from a diet full of sugar (charged energies) to a diet full of produce and superfoods (neutral energy and your own personal power). You will realize what you thought was love was just an attention high. You can expect your quality of life to improve and you may find yourself exercising greater mental flexibility. Now that you are properly nourished, you are better able to navigate life and relationships from a healthier place with more confidence, authenticity, and sustainability.

Chapter Summary

Your Grounding Cord tool helps you distinguish your energy from the energy of others. You now know how to visualize a grounding cord and how to channel unwanted energy in your space down your grounding cord. You can use your Grounding Cord tool to ground out colors that represent feelings, thoughts, people, or other frequencies that are not serving you.

There are three main steps to calming yourself with a grounding cord:

Step 1: Imagine a hollow tube near your hips that connects you to the Earth's center.

Step 2: Scan your energy field for colors or energies to send down your grounding cord that are charged and competing with your authenticity.

Step 3: Command, watch, feel, or trust that the colors, energies, and sensations are being sucked down your grounding cord where they are absorbed into the center of the Earth.

A grounding cord is most useful in moments when you find yourself overwhelmed or confused. It can really help you sort through your emotions. When you are overly affected by environmental energy, use your grounding cord to release all that is not yours and to get back to your most authentic self. If you are over-identifying with other people's emotions or feel inclined to take responsibility for their feelings or experiences, use your grounding cord to ground them out of your energy field. Your grounding cord is an ally you can rely on when you are feeling hyper, frantic, fragmented, nervous, or anxious. Call on your Grounding Cord tool any time you have something or someone to release.

It's always nice to fill in with a Golden Sun after a good grounding session. Think about it: With gravity running through your grounding cord, you are creating little vortex pockets with each color you release. The empty spaces can turn into invisible suction cups that will unconsciously suck environmental energies into your space, body, or aura. To prevent yourself from unconsciously filling in with unwanted energies, simply fill in consciously with your Golden Sun. When you see, feel, or experience yourself filling all the way up and in with your gold light, then you can rest assured that you are no longer vulnerable to environmental energies. There will be no room for them in your energy field.

Ground, Sun, and have fun! Make your cord your own and, above all, trust that energy follows intention! You are doing brilliant work!

SELF-ASSESSMENT

Ask yourself the following questions. On a scale of 1 to 5:

_____ *How relaxed am I feeling right now?* (Where 1 is "Ugh, I'm so annoyed; I feel like everything is in my way," and 5 is "Cool, calm, and collected.")

_____ *How easy is it for me to focus?* (Where 1 is "I feel like a million tabs are open," and 5 is "My mind is laser sharp.")

_____ *How is my emotional state?* (Where 1 is "I'm over-whelmed and confused," and 5 is "I feel at peace; all is well.")

_____ *How trusting am I feeling right now?* (Where 1 is "I'm freaking out! There's so much to do and so little time!" and 5 is "I know the universe has my back, and I can let go with ease.")

3
Preserving Your Personal Energy: Separation Tool

The sanctuary of the heart is no place
for the company of the antagonists.
—HAFIZ

Being Responsive to Life

It is no secret that modern society has conditioned us to be highly reactive to external stimuli. We have information coming at us from more angles and at a greater speed than at any other time in human history. With so many notification dings and all other kinds of information landing on our plates at any given moment, many of us feel compelled to react without taking the time to think first and respond second.

As you develop greater energetic awareness and develop a personal relationship with the tools in this book, you will start to notice your response to life changing. You will go from being *reactive* to being *responsive*.

Being *reactive* means we are matching the energy of our environment and engaging with it by throwing that same energy back at it. Because being reactive is so commonplace, most people don't realize just how disempowering it can be.

We often react subconsciously out of habit. Reacting is basically playing defense in life, which makes sense if we feel like our sense of calm is under threat. An example of reacting would be responding to a loud siren by screaming because it's loud and upsetting us. Another example of reacting might be suddenly feeling sad or frightened when we hear a siren, because we subconsciously know that sirens tend to signal someone needs help or has gotten very badly hurt. In both cases, our reactions match the environments in which we are situated, which means that the way we feel and live is highly determined, if not limited, by our surroundings. If we walk into a room of stressed-out people, we feel stressed. If we witness an angry parent scolding their child in the grocery store, we are overcome with emotion, whether it is anger, sadness, or disappointment. If this sounds familiar to you, know that your experience is more common than you'd think! Reacting is how we have been conditioned to live.

Absorbing this much can be very overwhelming. Without appropriate energetic boundaries, you could be unknowingly taking responsibility for everyone else's life experiences.

- Do you often experience highs and lows while listening to a story or scrolling on social media?

- Do you have a hard time setting boundaries? Maybe sometimes you feel bulldozed by life?

- Do your mood and thoughts fluctuate dramatically on a daily basis without you knowing exactly why this is happening?

Rest assured; the Separation tool is your new protective friend! In this chapter, you will be introduced to the Separation tool, which will help you become more responsive, rather than reactive, to the stimuli you receive daily. This chapter will help you develop your own Separation tool that you can deploy at any moment in any situation. Your Separation tool will help you preserve your personal energy so you can be the best version of you for yourself and the world!

SEPARATION TOOL AS MEDICINE	SEPARATION TOOL AS RITUAL
When you feel emotionally burnt out	Before leaving the house
If you feel compelled to say yes when your body is telling you no	Before beginning your work day
When you want to be present in a situation you might normally avoid	Before entering a crowded room
If you feel yourself over-empathizing with someone	Whenever separating two things, such as cutting something with a knife or scissors
When you want to be able to feel okay even when other people, near or far, are not feeling okay	Before hopping on social media

(CONTINUED)

SEPARATION TOOL AS MEDICINE	SEPARATION TOOL AS RITUAL
When you find yourself in the presence of a heated debate	Before entering a charged environment
If you feel like you are losing yourself to someone else's story or situation	Before going on a date
	When politics come up in conversation
	When you are getting dressed (You are adding a layer of separation between yourself and your environment physically, so why not do it energetically?)

In just a moment, you will be guided through the steps for the Separation tool. Before you begin, take a moment to assess how you are feeling right now.

SELF-ASSESSMENT

Ask yourself the following questions. On a scale of 1 to 5:

———   *How impressionable am I feeling right now?* (Where 1 is "I see it, I want it, I need it now!" and 5 is "I see it. I'm good. I'll think about it.")

———   *How strong are my boundaries right now?* (Where 1 is "I'm a total pushover," and 5 is "They are great and highly respected by all!")

———   *How influenced am I by what I read in the news and on social media about pain and suffering in the world?* (Where 1 is "I'm an energy sponge and can barely get out of bed," and 5 is "I am able to keep perspective so I have the energy to be the change I want to see in the world.")

_____ *How authentic am I feeling right now?* (Where 1 is "I don't even know who I am anymore; I feel like a chameleon," and 5 is "My actions reflect my values and beliefs.")

Visualizing

In a moment, you will allow your eyes to close and look within. Start slowing down your breath to begin box breathing as described here.

Inhale for four counts, then hold your breath for four counts, then exhale for four counts, and then hold for four counts. Repeat. Inhale for 4, 3, 2, 1; hold for 4, 3, 2, 1; exhale for 4, 3, 2, 1; hold for 4, 3, 2, 1.

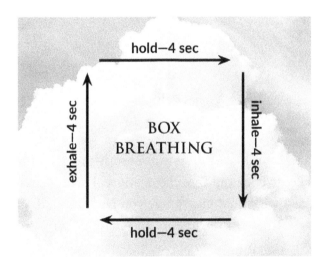

Visualize an object of your choice out in front of you. Most people enjoy the idea of a shield or some similar shape like a surfboard. I love to use plants, bushes, and trees. You may choose to use furniture, stuffed animals, or whatever else resonates with you. Picture this object hovering right in front of you at the edge of your aura. Two feet in front of you—about the length of your arm—is usually an effective distance. This object will absorb environmental energy so that you don't have to. Think of an object now.

If you haven't already done so, take a moment to close your eyes and visualize this object. Whatever it is, take a closer look at it with your mind's eye and trust whatever you see.

Great!

Separation tools are meant to absorb energy, rather than reflect energy back out into the universe. For this reason, the only object we would discourage you from using is a mirror. Separation tools help us reduce the chaos in our own space and serve as a protective shield in our response to our surrounding environments. It is best to visualize an object that can absorb energy. What object have you chosen as your Separation tool? If you don't like the object that you have chosen, go with something else that feels better.

In a moment, when you close your eyes again and imagine your Separation tool, take a closer look at it. Can you see it better? How large is it? What are its dimensions? What color is your Separation tool? Try to trust whatever images and colors first appear or come to mind. This will help you to hone your intuition and accept whatever comes up. This is you receiving your own intuitive information.

Always know, however, that you may manipulate the image or color if you so choose. What material is it made of? Can you spin it around to get a 360-degree view of it? See your Separation tool in as much detail as possible so that it looks so real to you that you can almost reach out and touch it.

Go ahead and close your eyes once again to take it in even more.

Beautiful! May this tool take on all the energy of your environment so that all that unwanted energy doesn't stick to you or compromise your intuition or authenticity.

As you continue to get acquainted with your Separation tool, feel free to open and close your eyes whenever and as much as you like. You know what works best for you.

Your Image

Before setting your Separation tool to work, please declare it as yours. Visualize placing an image of yourself inside your Separation tool to calibrate it to your own unique energy vibration. The image can be a real image of you or one you are imagining now. It is merely a placeholder, so as long as you are clear on what the image represents, you are all set!

Your Signature

You may write out your signature in the center of your Separation tool to reinforce that image of you and really make sure it is working for you and you alone. Now you are looking at your Separation tool in all of its glory, and it is reflecting your beaming face and your signature back at you. Perfect! Now to set it to work . . .

Orbiting and Absorbing

Now that you have owned your Separation tool, watch as it orbits around you, picking up and absorbing environmental energy and preventing it from affecting you. Maybe a loud, piercing siren of a fire truck is passing by; your Separation tool will absorb the alarm of the siren so that you don't. In this way, your Separation tool is able to absorb trauma that surrounds you. Notice how it moves with you as you walk through life. Perhaps a colleague or friend is passionately venting to you about something; your Separation tool allows you to remain neutral and compassionate while preventing you from going down their emotional rabbit hole. In this way you can be of better service to your friend. Think about it, wouldn't it be more helpful for you to stand your ground and help them out of the hole than to fall into the depths of despair with them? It keeps you in your space and in your position of power. Your Separation tool can even help you retain your power and groundedness when you expose your-self to charged information in the news, in a movie, or on social media.

Case Study

Brooke—From Emotional to Intentional

Brooke has always experienced intense feelings. She told me she often felt very sensitive and emotional. As an actor, she was able to channel her feelings into her roles, but she didn't always know what to do with them when she wasn't acting. She was unintentionally channeling other people's energy.

One day Brooke was driving to an audition. She was all pumped up and in a great mood. But while reciting her lines at a stop light, tears started running down her cheeks, and her heart started racing. She felt a mixture of upset, disappointment, and sadness and had no idea what was happening or why. Nor did she want to experience any of this just moments before her big audition. Brooke wiped her eyes, blasted some music, and recited her lines with conviction but still she could not escape this overwhelming feeling of anxiety, pain, and suffering.

When the light turned green, a car sped up next to her to pass her. She noticed that the couple in the car was fighting. Even though their windows were up, she could tell they were shouting because of their hand gestures and the way the car was rocking. One of them was crying, and they were both visibly upset. Brooke watched all of this for just a few seconds before they sped off into the distance. The farther their car got from her, the better she felt. Hope and optimism returned to her. The confidence and enthusiasm she had felt in her preparation for the audition resurfaced. It was in that moment that Brooke understood how problematic living without a Separation tool could be for her. She hadn't realized how much of an impact others' feelings could have on her. The intensity she had grown used to feeling was likely a build-up of other people's emotions.

For Brooke, a Separation tool was like having an "off" button. That same day, when she arrived at her audition, she sat in her car for a while and envisioned her Separation tool. She watched all the energy she had absorbed from the couple leave her space and enter her Separation tool. She felt better! She felt light and free.

During her audition, when she was receiving directives and feedback, she imagined all of that energy as colors flowing into her Separation tool and sparing her energy field. She took the comments in stride and was able to address them calmly and professionally. Historically, she would have taken such feedback more personally, but thanks to the upset couple, Brooke had utilized her Separation tool that day.

She got the part! Although that's not a surprise. The real victory is that Brooke is better able to focus on her work and talents without the distractions. She is unaffected by other people's opinions of her and is better able to receive feedback. Brooke has an easier time living in her body. The unwanted intensity in her life has disappeared.

Destroying and Creating

Just like your Grounding Cord tool, your Separation tool accumulates energy as it works for you and will need to be destroyed and re-created often. Built-up energy can limit the efficacy of the Separation tool, just as is the case when your grounding cord has built up too much energy. Destroy your Separation tool and create a new one as needed. Destroying can mean popping your tool, setting it on fire, making it explode, or erasing it. Do whatever it takes to make it disappear completely. For more emotionally taxing days, this can mean switching out multiple Separation tools over the course of the day. For example, if you have an especially charged interaction with a person, we recommend destroying your Separation tool immediately afterward and creating a new one.

Once you have destroyed your old Separation tool, go ahead and create a new one for yourself. It can be made out of the same material and look just like the last one, or you are welcome to explore different objects to serve the same purpose. Just remember to declare your Separation tool as uniquely yours by placing an image of yourself and your signature in it so it works for you and only you.

Wonderful! Welcome to your Separation tool!

 Accepting whatever comes up
is you honing your intuition.

Case Study

Albert—From Defensive to Directive

Albert had a defensive personality. Although he was an administrative assistant at a company that was extremely inclusive and supportive, every time he sat to get a simple task done, he would feel inadequate, too slow, like he had failed already. Before he even opened up an email in the morning he would feel a rush of anxiety and a nagging feeling that he was incapable of addressing the contents of the email.

Where did all this come from, he wondered? After all, Albert had only ever received praise from his team. As a child, however, Albert's parents were forever unsatisfied with him. His father would constantly berate him, and his mother was always worrying about him. Their opinions of him led him to think very little of himself.

He had been so used to disappointing his family's authority figures that he would feel shame whenever faced with authority. Whenever Albert's boss would point out something as simple as a typo, he would receive the feedback as harsh disappointment. He would feel like he was one mistake away from being fired no matter how far from his boss's mind that was. Albert always felt as if he was on the verge of imploding when he expected any feedback to be coming his way.

To work on these issues, Albert began to create a Separation tool. He would envision his parents' discouraging words as colors that his Separation tool would absorb. Albert had also received a lot of negative feedback from others—older siblings, teachers, employers—that he was holding on to. But now, all their words went into the Separation tool. Albert's favorite part of this visualization was when he threw the Separation tool into a dumpster fire. Kaboom! An explosion! A furious fire that destroyed all of that energy! Those hurtful words were all gone!

Next, Albert set up a new Separation tool to absorb all the colors and charged energy from his work day. He would eventually need to receive feedback, so he planned for his Separation tool to absorb all of the colors coming off his boss's words so he could better hear and receive the feedback. What he realized was that sometimes, when his boss would give him feedback or directives, the colors would come off of him rather than his boss. He would throw the negative self-talk into his Separation tool, as well.

Feedback no longer felt threatening to Albert. He started hearing his boss and teammates more clearly and receiving their emails with neutrality. He became less scared of "making mistakes" and more focused on mastering the job. He became more engaged in his job, taking directives and notes and asking questions all because his Separation tool helped him to not take things so personally.

Responding versus Reacting

The more you use your Separation tool, the better you will be able to respond to rather than react to environmental energy. Remember, *reacting* is that habit where you impulsively match the energy around you. *Responding*, on the other hand, is when your environment does not run the show. You run the show, and you are authentically yourself no matter the situation or setting.

Responding goes like this: Something happens, you give yourself time to process it, and only then do you respond to it from your authenticity. In responding, you are playing offense rather than defense in life. You are living life on purpose. You are doing what most affirms you. Your response will be a reflection of your truth. Imagine that when you hear sirens, you take a deep breath, further align yourself with your purpose, and keep on walking. With the Separation tool, life doesn't control you, you control life.

Your Separation tool absorbs environmental energy so it doesn't impact you. If the environmental energy affirms your truth, it will resonate within you in a way that supports your authenticity. If the environmental energy is in conflict with your truth, it will simply stay absorbed in your Separation tool so you remain unbothered by that energy frequency.

For example, when I first started working intentionally with my intuition, Tim had greater faith in me than I had in myself. I was mindful to keep my Separation tool up because boundaries had never been my strong suit, and I knew that as a novice, I was especially sensitive to what people might say about my intuitive readings. It was in those early years that I really understood the power of the Separation tool. I employed my Separation tool as a protective filter orbiting me; when pollutants such as words of pessimism regarding my psychic gifts came my way, my Separation tool absorbed them so I could continue to share my truth, completely unbothered.

The Separation tool also worked in my favor when Tim would sing my praises. My Separation tool would absorb all of Tim's energy; however, the sentiment behind his words of praise would make it through. I was in agreement with those words; they validated my truth. I already had those sentiments in my orbit, and Tim's words would just jog my memory and help me better access my own personal truth. Without my Separation tool, I may have felt like all my confidence was derived from Tim and not from within. I realized that Tim's truth simply affirmed my personal truth. The Separation tool allows compliments to be self-affirming rather than externally validating.

With your Separation tool engaged, whether you are receiving a compliment or an insult and whether you agree or disagree, you feel the same. There's great power in maintaining seniority in your energetic space. It allows for greater authenticity, clarity, courage, and self-expression. When you use this tool, you will not be easily influenced by your surroundings. Rather, each of your decisions, thoughts, feelings, and actions will be a reflection of your authentic light, values, and core beliefs. You will find it easier to stay aligned and live in integrity with yourself.

Multiple Separation Tools

Another option you have is to create multiple Separation tools. I use multiple Separation tools daily. This can be especially helpful for more sensitive situations in which you are more likely to feel triggered or extra vulnerable—for example, holidays, job interviews, performances.

You can create two, three, or even four Separation tools at a time and have all of them orbit around you. They can all look exactly the same or be different from one another. Create them in front of you as you normally would, own and declare them as uniquely yours, and then set them to orbit around you. You will notice that they tend to space themselves out, an equal distance apart, whether it's two, three, or four tools (or more).

Tim often reminds me how much he loves his Separation tool. He loves how calm and supported he feels when he imagines it. The very first one he visualized and used for years looked like a surfboard. He's not a surfer, but it was the first object that popped up, and it felt good enough, so he went with it.

When it came to an image of himself to choose, he thought about a happy picture of himself as a child that he could imagine clearly. He pictured it being hung on the inside of the surfboard, facing him. He also got in the habit of writing his signature with a big Sharpie in his most authentic, messy way on the surfboard.

Over time, your Separation tool may change form and may even change by the day. Tim's has shifted from a surfboard to a redwood tree to an enormous rock. Mine has shifted from my teddy bear to trees to bouquets of flowers. When practicing this new tool, you may begin by using just one Separation tool for the entire day. You might then try out seeing how it feels to use multiple Separation tools orbiting you throughout a day. Maybe even try out destroying old Separation tools and creating new ones every two to three hours in a given day.

When you experience the contrast between these different ways of using your Separation tool, you will better understand how it can be of greatest service to you and why. Feel free to ask yourself questions like *Why do I feel better on days when I use four Separation tools? Why do I take on more environmental energy in some contexts than others? Why do I have more energy when I create new Separation tools every two hours?*

Don't be afraid to be curious about what works best for you as this is a way of learning about yourself and what best serves you.

One of the coolest things we experience with our Separation tool is when it orbits quickly around us; it looks like there are many identical tools orbiting us all at once, creating what feels like a protective forcefield around us. With this experience, we can feel ourselves relaxing and letting down our guard with a bit more ease.

USING THE SEPARATION TOOL

Now take a moment to close your eyes and try to visualize the steps of the Separation tool on your own.

Step 1: Imagine an object of your choice about two feet in front of you. See it in as much detail as possible.

Step 2: Own your Separation tool by placing an image of yourself and your signature in the center of it so that it belongs to you and works for you alone.

Step 3: Set your Separation tool into orbit. As it circles you, it will absorb and collect environmental energy from around you so your energy field is free of environmental impact.

Integrity and Density

When first learning about the Separation tool, some people express concern over the gaps between the orbiting tools and whether there's a chance that environmental energy could seep through.

I always tell them that when I first learned about this tool, I would create multiple layers of them. I never left home without an entire forest of trees orbiting around me! I quickly started to realize, however, that it became a bit exhausting for me to maintain an entire forest. Can you imagine? Your Separation tools are as strong as you will them to be.

These days, I have only one layer of trees circling me, and it feels a little more peaceful and generally trusting. I've been doing this work for a while now, so my boundaries are better than ever, and the trees are taking care of themselves. Over time, I have repeatedly proven to myself that my Separation tools work, so it takes less and less effort to activate them. You will eventually find a balance that helps you feel secure. For now, may you be guided by whatever feels most safe in terms of maintaining healthy energetic boundaries.

Another concern Separation tool first-timers often have is about the density of their Separation tool—whether an object can be too thick or impermeable. You want to think of your Separation tool as a semipermeable membrane. If it is too permeable, you will be letting too much in. If this is the case, you may be highly reactive, easily influenced by your environment, and unusually emotional. At the other extreme, if it is impermeable, you will likely feel disconnected from life and could be withholding love and life from yourself. A semipermeable Separation tool offers you a buffer and helps maintain your authenticity and integrity, allowing you to think and feel for yourself.

The Separation tool is especially important for people who unintentionally become energy sponges.

When we don't use a Separation tool, we may unknowingly pick up on environmental energy, and our walk through life can become a series of knee-jerk reactions. We may find ourselves involved in a chain reaction of impulsive behavior—habits and patterns that we have not given much thought to. We project back out into the world all that we have absorbed from our environments. This reactive way of living is inauthentic and does not reflect our own truth.

With the help of your Separation tool, and the healthy energetic and psychological boundaries it offers you, you are better able to respond to life from a place of power, from your own value system and truths, rather than mirroring your environment back to itself. You become a lighthouse of your own energy rather than a sponge of energy that is not yours. Instead of being reactive in life, your Separation tool allows you to be proactive.

Case Study

Yasmine—From Empath to Intuitive

Yasmine was an unprotected psychic who was taking classes to hone her intuition. She had always known she was psychic. When hearing about other people's experiences, she would find herself on an emotional rollercoaster, as though the experiences were her own. She felt as though the emotional turmoil was a reflection of her psychic gifts and was actually proud to be able to merge energy fields with others as intimately. She was skeptical of having energetic boundaries, however, because she believed they would "block" or reduce her psychic abilities. If she didn't allow herself to feel others, how could she possibly tap into their energy to help them?

Yasmine was convinced the Separation tool wasn't for her and that she was a more effective psychic without it. She wanted to feel it all. The feelings validated her intuitive gifts and helped her feel more connected to people. That is, until she started getting migraines.

Yasmine was a skilled psychic, so the moment she started offering readings, she was in high demand. She went from offering an average of one psychic reading per month to offering several readings weekly, and sometimes several readings daily. The more readings she gave, the more likely it was that she would develop a migraine.

Multiple layers of Separation tools are great for people working professionally with energy work. Yasmine began to imagine a thick forest of trees orbiting her as her Separation tool. Until the migraines subsided, she created a new forest of Separation tools for each psychic session.

She found it a little tedious to visualize all of this each day. She was especially annoyed to have to take as much time in between sessions to set up a whole new Separation tool each time. When she was channeling, she was in a flow and didn't want it interrupted.

This is a case where an ounce of prevention is worth a pound of cure. When Yasmine took that extra ten minutes to destroy her old Separation tool and create a new one in between sessions, she saved herself hours' and days' worth of pain and increased her capacity for sessions.

Today Yasmine recognizes that her Separation tool actually enhances her psychic abilities; it doesn't take away from them. She doesn't rely on the rollercoaster ride of feelings to validate her intuition anymore. She maintains feelings of peace, calm, and trust within the sanctuary of her Separation tool and is now able to radiate that stillness outward for her clients' benefit.

Energetic Protection

Your Separation tool keeps you contained in your power, preventing your energy from leaking out and unwanted energy from coming in. It keeps you in the light, integrity, love, and higher vibrations of all experiences and protects you from lower-level energies that distract you from your light. Light attracts light. Light recognizes light. Your Separation tool keeps you in your light so that you are better equipped to connect with the light that surrounds you and to offer light to your surroundings.

I use the words *light* and *dark* or *higher* and *lower* energies simply to illustrate how energy works. The truth is, energy doesn't necessarily possess any color—but we use colors to perceive different energies—nor does energy judge or display an affinity for one kind of energy or another. Energy just is. Culturally, we tend to associate goodness with light and evil with darkness, but nothing is inherently good about light or evil about darkness. So when I contrast lower-level energies with light/lightness/higher-level energies, I am simply referring to energies that you perceive to be unproductive or harmful to you and energies you perceive to be beneficial or advantageous to you, respectively.

Your Separation tool absorbs environmental energy that is not in alignment with yours and would otherwise compromise your energy. It is not about good or bad. It is about what reinforces your light, your spirit, or your own personal truths and values. That which assists you on your own unique path on this planet—which is completely different from everyone else's. And it's that difference that reinforces your soul's purpose. Anything that's not reinforcing your soul's purpose distracts from and can slow down your ability to realize your highest potential. Your Separation tool absorbs all of that external energy so you may reach your highest potential in peace.

Ever feel like some people are standing a little too close, even when they are ten feet away from you? Or have you ever felt violated or attacked just by another person's vibe? Have you noticed that when some people in your life are in a bad mood, you can't help but be bummed out too?

This experience is common with empaths, highly sensitive people, and virtually anyone in a profession in which part of their job involves trying to understand and/or help others. When empathizing with others is such a big part of our lives, we can easily become derailed by environmental energy and confuse it with our own.

Without a Separation tool, you might find yourself walking down the street thinking, "I need pizza," as you catch a whiff when passing by a pizza stand, and "ooh, I wanna watch that new show," as you pass by a billboard, and "omg, I gotta get into roller skating," when you pass by a group of people having fun skating around. With your Separation tool, you will see all those wonderful things and even admire them, but you won't feel an emotional pull. If you are not hungry, you're more likely to think, "I love pizza," or just "hmm."

Regarding the show, maybe you just say, "aww," or when you admire the roller skaters, maybe you just smile.

Your Separation tool removes those emotional attachments and judgments from your observations. All the "shoulds," "needs," "goods," and "bads" are filtered through your Separation tool so that everything just is. Pizza just is. The show just is. Roller skating just is.

Similarly, when a colleague tells you their opinion about something, it just is. It's not immediately influential. Everything becomes information and feedback that you can use. As they speak to you, you can envision their energy as a color or their very words might be absorbed by your Separation tool. You still receive the information, only without it having an impact on your energy. It just is. This way, you get to take a pause, breathe normally, observe, and more calmly decide what you would like to do with that information. It can just remain in your Separation tool where it won't have the power to impact your thoughts, feelings, actions, or opinions.

Energy Adjusts Accordingly

The more you get into the habit of deploying your Separation tool, the easier it will be to visualize and the more often it will fade into the background as it continues to work for you. This is fine, as energy adjusts itself accordingly. What we pay attention to will grow; conversely, what we neglect will disappear. Depending on your relationship with the Separation tool, it can take anywhere from three to seven days for it to dissolve completely after you initially create it. It first accumulates energy, thus reducing its efficacy to the point where it simply becomes a rotating object and loses its purpose as a Separation tool. At that point, it will dissolve back into the universe where it came from.

So, if you forget about your Separation tool, that's fine. It will take care of itself. It will eventually get reabsorbed back into the universe, and the energy will go back into circulation. The important question is this: Will you remember to create yourself a new Separation tool?

Like most of these tools, the longer you use it, the more powerful it becomes. You will start to trust it more after you get some feedback from it, thereby empowering it more. It will also be more effective with time. But it is like brushing your teeth—the effects only last so long. For maximum efficacy, it is best to make it a regular practice.

A good practice to get into is creating a new Separation tool every day, maybe even at the same time and same location. This will help you create a ritual that you can come back to. Sure, some days will call for more Separation tools at different points in your day, and if it's one of those days, you can easily create a second or third one. And remember, if you are feeling overwhelmed by your environment, you can always destroy the old Separation tool and create as many new ones to orbit around you as you wish.

If you make this a daily practice, you will start doing it on autopilot so you can feel safe and authentically you as much as possible.

By now you have had some practice closing your eyes and visualizing. A big question I had when I began this work was how to distinguish between images that would simply appear and those that I would consciously manipulate.

In general, you will want to receive whatever first comes to you. This is your intuition speaking. By accepting what comes to you, you are "seeing like an anthropologist," allowing whatever is to just be what it is, which becomes easier and easier with practice.

Additionally, the image you receive can serve as a message for you to investigate further. Let's say you notice a hole in your grounding cord. You can ask yourself, *Why is there a hole?* Perhaps the hole signifies that your intuition is trying to reveal something about your relationship to feeling grounded or being able to feel a greater sense of peace in your life. Or imagine that one day your Separation tool is zipping around you really quickly compared to another day when it seemed to be moving very slowly. You can ask yourself what this difference might suggest and trust what messages come up. Observing the initial images that you are receiving can be very informative, for this is you honing your intuitive abilities, your ability to see clearly and to receive insight in the form of images. Please be curious about all you are witnessing and ask questions to see what the answers unveil.

This energetic healing can benefit your cardiovascular health, your blood pressure, your nervous system, your sleep, and more. You can use this type of healing with all the tools in this book. With regard to the Separation tool in particular, if you are not loving the tool you first envisioned, simply swap it out for a new one, thereby healing your relationship with boundaries and authenticity.

  Manipulating images is important because it is a way of healing yourself, reinforcing your power, and understanding that you are the conscious creator of your own life and reality. Receiving and altering images are interdependent processes and can be equally useful.

Manipulating the images is something to try when you want to heal yourself. After your intuition offers you insight, you have the power both to heal and create a new reality for yourself. If, for example, you see holes or rips in the grounding cord, you can heal yourself by mending them. Since the mind, body, and spirit are all one, when you mend them, you are healing your relationship with peace and stillness and are receiving so much more than that which the grounding cord represents.

Case Study

Vivian—From Panic to Presence

Vivian tended to over-identify with suffering. When Vivian was in graduate school, she found that she often lacked energetic boundaries and needed to engage her Separation tool.

Once, Vivian attended a lecture being given by a famous intellectual that she greatly revered. She sat on the edge of her seat, listening to the speaker's every word and trying to make sense of her complicated talk. At some point, Vivian noticed that one of her very smart friends who happened to be sitting next to her was formulating a question to ask the speaker. Without even noticing it, Vivian suddenly became very nervous. Her breathing became shallower, her muscles tightened, and her palms began to sweat. She suddenly realized she was taking on her friend's nervous energy.

Why do I care if he asks a question? Why should I be intimidated? This has nothing to do with me! Vivian thought. She stopped herself, visualized removing his energy from her space and engaging her Separation tool, and immediately she felt like herself again.

Especially for empaths, over-identifying with others happens all the time. We listen to a reporter speak about something terrible that has happened, and we can feel it in our bodies, even if the event has no direct impact on us. Moments like these are perfect for engaging the Separation tool.

Vivian decided to start each day with a new Separation tool. She loved it! When studying with classmates, she no longer felt like she was taking on their stress or fears. When unwinding with friends, she no longer felt like she was taking on their body image stuff. She realized just how sensitive she had always been to what other people were experiencing and how stifling that was for her.

With her Separation tool, Vivian was better able to be present. She used to find the experiences of others invasive, so she sometimes came across as defensive or distant. With her Separation tool engaged, she was able to listen to her friends or colleagues vent and recognize her experience as different than theirs. She was able to feel calm and cool even when others were uncomfortable.

Separation Tool Synergy

By now you have learned about your Golden Sun tool, your Grounding Cord tool, and the Separation tool. Each of these work synergistically together to reinforce one another.

- You regain your personal power with your Golden Sun tool.

- Your Separation tool allows you to maintain that power and prevent it from leaking out.

- You release charged and unwanted energies in your space with your Grounding Cord tool.

- Your Separation tool also helps prevent a good amount of those unwanted energies from coming into your energy field in the first place. You will start to notice that you have a lot less to ground out when you are employing your Separation tool.

As your relationship with your Separation tool grows, so will your self-understanding and self-awareness. As with all the tools, your Separation tool is both a diagnostic and a healing modality.

Diagnostically speaking, take note of when you feel you need many Separation tools or when they are filling up fast. You may feel better around some people, experiences, or environments when you employ more Separation tools. Is it sustainable for you to employ many Separation tools to feel comfortable with such people or places or would you rather conserve your energy and focus on experiences that don't require as many Separation tools? With practice you will discover what works best for you.

Chapter Summary

Your Separation tool distinguishes where you end and the world begins. It helps you stay contained in your energy field and preserves your personal energy so you don't feel drained. It helps you maintain your authenticity so all you think, feel, do, and say is a reflection of your beliefs and values. The energetic boundaries it provides help you respond to life from your unique and authentic Golden Sun energy. With your Separation tool spinning around you, you will have an easier time focusing on yourself and not getting distracted by the lives of others.

You now know how to create a Separation tool, calibrate it to best serve you, set it in orbit, and destroy it. You are all set to exercise your energetic boundaries!

Remember the three steps you can take to create energetic boundaries with your Separation tool:

Step 1: Imagine an object of your choice about two feet in front of you. See it in as much detail as possible.

Step 2: Own your Separation tool by placing an image of yourself and your signature in the center of it so that it belongs to you and works for you alone.

Step 3: Set your Separation tool into orbit. As it circles you, it will absorb and collect environmental energy so your energy field remains free of environmental impact.

A Separation tool works best as preventative medicine. Start off by creating a new one each day so you can take your aura of authenticity and integrity with you everywhere you go. This is a powerful tool to use if you tend to have a hard time maintaining healthy boundaries. If you ever feel that your boundaries are slipping, simply destroy your Separation tool and create a whole new one. Swap Separation tools out as needed.

Use your Separation tool to help you distinguish between your emotions and those of other people and contexts. If you find yourself overwhelmed by the energy of a particular person or situation, imagine that energy as a color that gets absorbed by your Separation tool, and then notice that your space is clear of that energy. Use your Separation tool when you are feeling extra vulnerable, overly sensitive, or emotional. It's helpful when you want to listen to others without taking on their energy.

You are divinely protected. May your boundaries offer you greater safety and freedom in self-expression. Have fun with this tool, make it your own, and above all, trust that energy follows intention!

SELF-ASSESSMENT

Ask yourself these questions. On a scale of 1 to 5:

_____   *How impressionable am I feeling right now?* (Where 1 is "I see it, I want it, I need it now!" and 5 is "I see it. I'm good. I'll think about it.")

_____   *How strong are my boundaries right now?* (Where 1 is "I'm a total pushover," and 5 is "They are great and highly respected by all!")

_____   *How influenced am I by what I read in the news and on social media about pain and suffering in the world?* (Where 1 is "I'm an energy sponge and can barely get out of bed," and 5 is "I am able to keep perspective so I have the energy to be the change I want to see in the world.")

_____   *How authentic am I feeling right now?* (Where 1 is "I don't even know who I am anymore; I feel like a chameleon," and 5 is "My actions reflect my values and beliefs.")

4
Dwelling in Your Power: Center of Your Head Tool

Every moment
With you
I'm falling in love
Anew.
—HAFIZ

Your Neutral Inner World

Living in a growth and goal-oriented society sets us up to become attached to outcomes. Goals help us organize our thoughts, develop plans, and take action. Goals can be great for us! Goals can also cause us to lose sight of the bigger picture, which can get us into trouble. Too much attachment to outcomes can cause us to develop tunnel vision, dig in our heels, or make us stubborn enough to go down with a sinking ship.

In this chapter, you will become acquainted with the Center of Your Head tool. It is a special tool that can get you to a place where all is well and everything happens for a reason. It is what you will use to tap into your intuition for greater trust in the process of life.

When you are in the center of your head, you feel calm, as though you are in the observer's seat. You are able to watch the story of life unfold without any attachment to the outcome of the story or any agenda for the main character. The center of your head is your place of neutrality. Some would call it the *seat of your soul*.

 Decisions made from the center of your head will reflect your values and facilitate self-actualization with much grace, peace, and flow.

The Center of Your Head tool helps you zoom out to get a greater perspective. From this vantage, you will see your goals differently. Henry David Thoreau explained it well when he said, "What you get by achieving your goals is not as important as what you become by achieving your goals." It's all about the bigger picture, and the center of your head is where it's at.

We have been placing a lot of emphasis on neutrality up until now, and it has all led to this moment. The center of your head is also known as your sixth chakra, your third eye, your brow chakra, or your psychic chakra. It is where your intuition resides. Neutrality is what provides you with access to your intuition. The center of your head is naturally neutral, so just by virtue of existing there, you are less inclined to be reactive and more open to listening to the whispers of your intuition with an underlying sense of trust.

The center of your head is where you can go to get all your intuitive information. For example,

- Do you sometimes feel that there are too many conflicting voices in your head? Do you experience inner conflict when making decisions?

- Do you experience doubt, confusion, or cyclic thoughts? Do you wonder what other people are thinking of you or what impression you just made?

- Do you have intuitive moments that come and go and you are not sure why or when the inspiration will strike?

Today is your lucky day! Welcome to the center of your head!

In this chapter you will learn how to create a custom-fit neutral space to dwell in, to see reality as it is, to explore the spiritual significance of it all, and to become aligned with your highest self. You will return to this, your own special place, time and time again to gain clarity, confidence, and an elevated perspective. Doing so will require practice at first, but eventually, you will find yourself spending longer and longer periods of time here, where all is well and where everything happens for a reason.

CENTER OF YOUR HEAD TOOL AS MEDICINE	CENTER OF YOUR HEAD TOOL AS RITUAL
When you are overwhelmed with emotion and need clarity	Every morning, when you get out of bed
If you are feeling low, doubtful, or suspicious	When you begin your work day.
When you experience internal conflict about something	Before entertaining the opinions of others
If you feel jealous or envious of others	When using any form of transportation
When you want to surrender to the feeling of trust	Before getting into something creative
When you need a safe space that affirms your existence in the most tender way	Whenever you pass by your altar

In just a moment, you will be guided through the steps for the Center of Your Head tool. Before you begin, take a moment to assess how you are feeling right now.

SELF-ASSESSMENT

Ask yourself these questions. On a scale of 1 to 5:

_____   *How conflicted am I feeling?* (Where 1 is "My head is spinning; I'm confused, hazy, and foggy," and 5 is "I am clear as can be about my feelings.")

_____   *How much am I trusting the process of life right now?* (Where 1 is "I don't want to trust, I want absolute power and control," and 5 is "It is what it is, and it's all working out in divine order whether it feels like it or not.")

_____   *How self-confident are you feeling?* (Where 1 is "I'm full of doubt, often feel imposter syndrome, and am over-critical of myself," and 5 is "I love and accept myself exactly as I am.")

_____   *How empowered is your perspective?* (Where 1 is "Why is everything happening to me?" and 5 is "I see how everything is happening for me.")

Visualizing

Time to visualize!

Once again, you will allow your eyes to close and look within. Start slowing down your breath to begin box breathing as described here.

Inhale for four counts, then hold your breath for four counts, then exhale for four counts, and then hold for four counts. Repeat. Inhale for 4, 3, 2, 1; hold for 4, 3, 2, 1; exhale for 4, 3, 2, 1; hold for 4, 3, 2, 1.

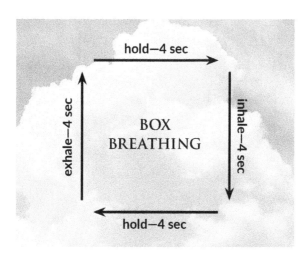

Now start focusing all your awareness and your energy quite literally to the center of your head—the space between your ears and behind your eyes. This is the location of your sixth chakra, which is commonly referred to as the third eye. Energetically speaking, this is your intuition space. You may tap above your ears or in between your eyes to draw all of your energetic attention here.

> " When your energy resides at the center of your head, you are instantaneously more connected with your intuition and authenticity. "

Start to envision a safe, sacred, and beautiful vista right there at the center of your head. Visualize a serene location where your soul can reside and where you will want to return repeatedly. This is where you will come to tap into all of your answers, which means you are naturally trusting the experience of being here.

To develop the center of your head, which will be your very own special place, you can imagine somewhere you have been before or you can make it up as you go. You might envision your favorite cabin in the woods, your living room, a beach, or a location your body has yet to experience. Take a moment now to close your eyes and visualize the center of your head.

How did it go?

You are in the center of your head! Welcome! You have arrived!

Please remember to be gentle with yourself and accept whatever comes up. Believe it or not, by doing this, you are actually honing your intuition. It's not about getting it right. Rather, it's about acceptance and allowance.

At the center of your head, time and space expand exponentially. Many people spending time in this place feel immersed in an expansive landscape. It works kind of like Mary Poppins's bag in the sense that this location is not limited to the measurements or confines of your skull—it can be as wide and spacious as you like. When you visualize the center of your head, really go there and imagine it in as much detail as possible. Remember, imagination and intuition work hand in hand and are very closely related.

Whatever you imagine, take it all in. What colors are present? What is in the foreground? What is in the background? Can you get a 360-degree view of the center of your head?

Open up all of your senses. What does it smell like in the center of your head? What does it sound like? Are you seated on a rock in the middle of the ocean listening to waves crashing, tasting the salt water, and feeling a cool breeze on your hot skin? Are you high on a mountain top where you can see trees going on to the horizon and can almost catch a whiff of pine? What temperature is it in the center of your head? What time of day is it?

CENTER OF YOUR HEAD TOOL

Go ahead and close your eyes again and try to imagine the center of your head in as much detail as possible. As always, take it easy and have fun!

Step 1: Concentrate your awareness to the center of your head, between your ears and behind your eyes.

Step 2: Observe the beautiful vista, engaging all of your senses.

Step 3: Look for your highest self, which exists in the center of your head.

Step 4: Have a seat in the center of your head and tune in to your intuition.

Too much, Too little, Just right.

Some students experience a flurry of images coming in when they close their eyes to visualize and have a hard time keeping up with them or manipulating them. Others see very little at first. Both experiences are very common and completely valid. Every person's experience of visualizing and honing their intuition is unique. There is no "right" or "wrong" way of visualizing. We are still in the beginning stages of constructing this sacred space for you, so take it all in stride.

After all, you are the ultimate creator here, and you are welcome to modify and redecorate the center of your head as needed until it feels right. Experiment! Feel free to try on different locations, colors, and textures for size. See about letting it be nighttime in the center of your head, and then the next time you return there, try making it daytime.

Eventually, you will want to decide on a setting you prefer and stick with one relatively consistent scene. Spend some time in the center of your head until you are able to choose a scene that most reinforces feelings of trust and surrender. Over the years, your preference for this space may change as you change, but most people prefer just one location for their lifetimes. Eventually you won't be able to get enough of this place and will look forward to coming back frequently.

In order to remain neutral, make sure that you are the only living being in the center of your head. While loved ones and pets are great and can absolutely make us happy, they can also take us out of a state of neutrality, which would be counterproductive here. Inevitably, my dog always finds his way into the center of my head. I love him so much! I would do anything for him, and he makes my heart sing. This is a fantastic feeling to experience, so fantastic that I want it to never end. The very fact that I want this feeling to last is why it is interfering with my neutrality and intuition. With my dog in the center of my head, I have a bias, a desire, and an agenda. I won't be able to see reality as it is through this biased lens. It is for that reason that I ground out my dog and any living beings from the center of my head. How do I do it? I simply send them down my trap door!

Your Trap Door

The next time you close your eyes, take a look around the center of your head for a trap door. Yep, just like one on a stage where things go to disappear. Scan the grounds for a door that blends seamlessly into the environment, and you will find it. Most people find theirs somewhere beneath their seat. When you pull up on the trap door, you will see a chute or a tube inside that connects with your grounding cord. It is almost like a smaller trash chute that connects to the bigger one—your grounding cord—that ultimately connects down into the Earth's center.

You will use this trap door much like you would your grounding cord. You will release any interference energy into it—any biases, inner conflict, charged energy, agendas, or desires—let them go down through your trap door, into your grounding cord, to the center of the Earth where they will be repurposed for better use. As you have been doing with your grounding cord, you may see these energies as colors leaving the center of your head. You may feel them leave, or you may simply know and trust that you are releasing them down your trap door. Either way is great!

If you have any people or pets in the center of your head, send them down your trap door, too; remember any living being in the center of your head will interfere with your neutrality and intuition. By sending them down your grounding cord, you release these beings from your space and give them their personal power back, which may result in them feeling an energy boost or sensation of alignment. Everyone wins!

Releasing all charges and beings from the center of your head aligns this space with your vibration, which reinforces your authenticity, your personal power, and your intuition. Unlike your grounding cord, which best serves you when it is attached to you with a gentle suction, you can use your trap door more like you do the vacuum hose when you are cleaning your house. You can send all unwanted energies and images down your trap door as necessary. You can do this daily or weekly. Once you have cleared this space of unwanted energies, please close the trap door and enjoy!

Neutrality

For someone to be neutral, they must lack strong opinions and feelings and not be attached to outcomes. For example, if your friend tells you they spank their child as a form of discipline, being neutral would be witnessing and listening without opinions, judgment, or feelings. A neutral state of mind lacks knee-jerk reactions and past associations with the topic at hand. When you are not in a neutral state and have strong feelings or opinions, your ability to clearly receive and translate intuitive messages is compromised.

Energy doesn't assign value to experiences or judge things to be right or wrong. When neutral, you are out of your ego-identity mind and better connected with your energy field and the energy in the room, which is why it helps reinforce your intuition. Let's return to the example of your friend telling you about how they spank their child: When you are neutral, you see *spanking* as a verb like any other verb rather than seeing it as something that is good or bad. From this place of neutrality, you are better able to see the big picture and address this disciplinary philosophy from your seat of neutrality rather than from a place of judgment.

*

The Center of Your Head tool is truly a precious gift. The more you close your eyes to visualize it and take time to notice how relaxed and safe it makes you feel, the more you will come to see this as an actual place where you can go. You will develop an association with it that will cause you to feel relaxed and at peace when you imagine it. The Center of Your Head tool can be a godsend when you need a moment to yourself or to get some perspective.

The landscapes that Tim and I have built in the center of our heads are pretty consistent, generally speaking. At the center of my head, I am seated on a comfy rock in the middle of the ocean. At the center of Tim's head, he is positioned on a high mountain plateau overlooking a vast landscape of trees. His seat is made of polished stone carved right out of the mountain. Even though both of our seats are made of rock, they are comforting and hold us perfectly when we sit on them.

When Tim goes to the center of his head, most often it appears to be dusk, but the colors vary. The sky might appear anywhere from orange to deep purple, the trees may look vibrant green, greenish brown, or almost black. It used to be daytime in the center of my head, but lately it's been right around sunset.

At times, our other senses get activated at the center of our heads—we hear water, smell trees, or catch a whiff of smoke from somewhere off in the distance. Trust whatever you experience when you go there. Allow yourself to acknowledge what feels good to you when you are there as this will reinforce the importance in this space.

Tim reminds me that at some point he began to notice that when he would first arrive at the center of his head, he would make some small adjustments—for instance, he'd smooth out some cracks in the rocks or light a few candles around his seat. Doing this helped him to claim that space as his; it made it just right for him.

"As an anthropologist who studies the universal human desire for belonging, I can attest that when people feel a sense of belonging, whether to a community or a place, they are better able to reach their highest potential," Tim points out. It makes perfect sense, then, that imagining a special place that is just right for us would provide us with a sense of belonging, and therefore, greater calm, less charge, and more neutrality.

 From the center of your head, all is well, and everything happens for a reason.

Case Study

Chad—From Annoying to Accepting

Chad was always trying to change others. As a student of acupuncture, he was eager to heal everyone. He married Hector before starting graduate school, and at first they had a wonderful marriage. However, the more Chad learned in school, the more he tried to apply what he learned to heal Hector. When he began studying mental health, Chad diagnosed Hector with depression and became adamant about treating him with a number of different herbal formulas. Similarly, when he was studying pain management, Chad became excited to treat Hector's back pain with cupping and acupuncture. This pattern repeated: Chad would inevitably find a new diagnosis for Hector and impose a treatment on him.

Hector finally had enough. He didn't enjoy being Chad's guinea pig, and more importantly, he didn't appreciate Chad's incessant desire to change him. "Why can't you just accept me as I am?" Hector would beg. But Chad continued to look for all of Hector's ailments—he had tunnel vision.

Although it appeared that Chad's actions were done out of love—he wanted his husband to be the best version of himself he could be—an agenda was involved, which signaled a lack of neutrality. Remember how love is energetically neutral? Well, if it's not love, then it's charged energy, and charged energy can manifest as judgment.

Here Chad was—in school, self-improving, and implementing all he learned. *Why doesn't Hector want to change and grow too?* Chad thought. *Why does he want to remain stuck in his old ways? Why can't he see I am just trying to help? And how will I be able to feel in sync with my partner if he doesn't change with me as I grow and change? What if I outgrow him in the process?*

Enter the Center of Your Head tool. Chad began to learn how to observe his marriage and power dynamics from the center of his head. When in the center of his head, Chad felt so calm and peaceful—like he had no problems at all. His laser-focused spotlight on Hector's imbalances zoomed out, and Chad was better able to see all of Hector's light. Chad began accepting and embracing Hector for all he brought to the table. From the center of his head, Chad realized that he *did* have an agenda for Hector. Before, Chad had thought that he wanted Hector to grow up and self-improve. However, when Chad went to the center of his head, he gained a different perspective and was able to realize that what he really wanted was validation from Hector.

Chad wanted Hector to tell him what a magnificent healer he was. If Chad could take responsibility for Hector's radically improving health, he would feel more confident in his new career path. Chad was shocked to learn this about himself. From this elevated perspective, he realized that his approach to healing Hector was really about his own insecurities. Chad decided to stop practicing on Hector and simply share with him all he learned each day. After this change, Chad discovered that Hector loved hearing about his adventures in acupuncture school and was happy to reflect back to him what a great practitioner he would be. The less smothered Hector felt, the more willing he was to ask Chad for advice, which, naturally, Chad loved!

Before developing the center of his head, Chad was trying to help Hector from the place of his own ego—the locus of power and control. After developing the center of his head, Chad was better able to see Hector as perfect, whole, and complete. From that point forward, helping Hector from the center of Chad's head was much easier and more empowering for both of them.

For example, Chad would treat Hector's headaches without any attachment to the outcome—he trusted that learning acupuncture was for his own personal gain regardless of whether his husband's headaches resolved. From the center of his head, Chad was better able to allow Hector his own karma, and he trusted that if the pain persisted, there must be a lesson in it *for Hector* rather than for himself.

The Center of Your Head tool taps us into spirit and is all about trust. Before becoming acquainted with the center of his head, Chad was treating Hector from a place of insecurity, nervousness, and a desire to impress. Chad wasn't trusting himself, and it was palpable. Once he started behaving in alignment with trust, Chad's world started reflecting trust back to him. His husband started trusting him as a practitioner rather than being put off by Chad's desire to "control him," as Hector put it. Chad's treatments transformed from ego to spirit and began bringing Hector and Chad closer together rather than separating them.

Let's dip back into the visualization. Return to the center of your head and take it all in: all the colors, the imagery, the sounds, and feelings. Create it in as much detail as possible so that it is real to you and easy for you to come back to over and over again.

 The center of your head is a serene environment where all is well, everything happens for a reason, and you are tapped into all those reasons. You are tapped into that realm of infinite possibilities.

Note any of the smells, sounds, and sensations that come up. Is there wind blowing in the trees? Is the sun kissing your skin? Does it smell like the ocean? Can you smell fresh cut grass? Whatever it may be, just engage all the senses and be right here, right now. And again, try to get that 360 view and try to see this place in as much detail as possible.

Please feel free to open or close your eyes, whenever doing so feels right, from now through the remainder of the chapter.

By now you have done the box breathing each time you have been introduced to a new tool. This practice is extremely powerful. It activates your parasympathetic nervous system, telling your body and mind that it is safe to relax.

When we repeatedly breathe this way, we become more and more relaxed. When we are relaxed, we are likely to respond from a place of peace and neutrality. It makes sense, right? When we chill out, all the little things that were bothering us before can more easily melt away. On the other hand, when we are stressed, it's so much easier to react without thinking or to say something we don't mean.

Bottom line: This very basic form of breathwork puts us into something of a trance state, where we can actively participate in visualizing. By visualizing, we largely mean following the prompts and accepting whatever comes up.

Every person relates differently to breathwork. For Tim, breathing into this relaxed state has helped him receive, accept, and learn from the visualizations. When he doesn't take the time to do this breathing before closing his eyes to visualize, the images and any information he gleans tend to be almost choppy with interference.

For this reason, especially when you are just beginning to use these tools, we highly recommend you take the time to do this breathwork and become relaxed before visualizing. It will be a better use of your time on so many levels. You will become more at ease, more energetically focused, and more neutral about the images and information that come up.

On a side note, you can also do this kind of breathing to help yourself fall asleep, but save that for later. For now, just get relaxed and go on this visual journey.

Your Highest Self

Now that you are familiar with the center of your head, it's time to meet the version of you that resides there—your most intuitive self, your spirit, the part of you that is tapped in! Allow this miniature version of you to look like whatever best represents your highest self.

Remember how some folks refer to this place as being the seat of your soul? Well, the you that lives in the seat of your soul is the you that knows you are here on Earth for a purpose. It is the you that existed before any parts of the human experience reached you—before you experienced any

suffering, disappointment, trauma, praise, or external validation. We will call this version of you your *highest self*. This is
your most intuitive, trusting, and authentic self.

What do you look like in the center of your head? For
most of you, you will find that you look similar to how you
look in human form, only in miniature, about one to two
inches tall. That said, some students are pleased to witness
themselves in animal form in the center of their heads. When
I first met my highest self, I was delighted to find that in the
center of my head I have gold skin, purple eyes, and super
long hair! At the center of Tim's head, he looks pretty much
the same, only a little taller with redder hair.

Remember, this is *your* intuitive space. It is custom-designed
for your neutrality and as a portal to your answers. If you are
having a hard time visualizing your highest self here, know
that you have all the power and authority to create this image
of you for yourself.

Just like you have been doing with your Grounding Cord
tool and Separation tool, try on a few different versions of
your highest self until you find the right one. You may even
recall a photo or two of yourself that you know and like.
What you perceive as your highest self ought to fill you up
with self-confidence, peace, and trust. For most of us, our
highest self will inspire bliss, joy, and feelings of connection
or euphoria. Play around with this image until you find a rep-
resentative of your soul that resonates with you and feels like
a natural fit that is easy to connect with repeatedly.

You may appear like your human self, a slight variation
of your human self, or nothing at all like your human form.
You will know and feel when you have met your highest
self because this little being will feel cozy, comfortable, and
inviting.

Case Study

Jennifer—From Smooshed to Spacious

Jennifer, a working single parent, felt she never had any time for herself. She had two jobs, two kids and, generally, too many people and things taking up her mental space. She experienced cyclical thoughts, was often worried about the smallest of things, and was prone to resenting others. Not only could Jennifer not seem to find any space for herself; more often than not, she felt crowded out of the space she did have. Her life felt cramped and rushed, causing her much anxiety.

When Jennifer started regularly practicing existing in the center of her head, like most students, she would close her eyes to get to that serene place and feeling. With time and practice, it would take Jennifer less time to get there with her eyes closed; eventually, with her eyes open, she began to superimpose the center of her head onto any location that she was in. The center of Jennifer's head was now easy for her to access at her two jobs, at her kids' schools, and at the park down the street.

This practice has helped Jennifer tremendously; she no longer sweats the small stuff. She has stopped fighting with her kids and has become better able to be a voice of reason for them. She can see much more clearly through the conflicts at her places of employment, which has helped her not to take work politics as personally. Overall, she feels more peaceful and trusting in how her life is unfolding. Her day-to-day activities haven't changed much, but her approach to them has, which has made all the difference. Now, Jennifer is much happier and more focused on her blessings than her grievances.

Owning the Center of Your Head

In addition to identifying with your highest self, another thing you can do to reinforce the efficacy of the center of your head is to *own* it. Remember how you owned your Golden Sun and Separation tools by writing your name in the center of them to indicate that they belong to you and can best support you? To own the center of your head, simply imagine yourself doing what you love to do most. That's right. Your favorite activity. It is so fun!

Have you ever noticed how when you are doing what you love, time almost stops and you don't have a care in the world? Whether it's biking, cooking, dancing, painting, writing, running, or another activity, it feels like you are in the flow of things, and everything is close to perfect. It's as if your life is a daydream, and you are the "whole universe in ecstatic motion," as Rumi might say.

Now bring *that* energy to the center of your head! Why? Because when we are doing what we love, we are the most tapped into energy. It is during these moments that we think less and consciously exist more.

> The center of your head is where you will go to focus on the journey, not the destination. It is where you will become powerfully present, unattached to outcome and energies of the past or the future.

When your highest self practices your favorite activity in the center of your head, you own this space as being uniquely yours. You affirm that this space is your safe space where you can surrender to your highest self. You accept that this space will bring you back to neutrality, intuition, and flow each time you visit it. You set the frequency of this location to your unique vibration so that it is a location that only you have access to; this will make it so it is of utmost support to you.

Enjoy being your highest self doing your most favorite thing in the center of your head whether it is hiking, laughing, jumping, building things, designing things, or doing somersaults. The only activity you will want to avoid is one that requires another being, even if it's your pet, as that requires you to interact with energy that is not yours. Think of an activity that involves you and only you, and reserve playing fetch with Bubba for later.

How does it feel to do your favorite activity here? Can you see why Tim and I never want to leave this place?

Take a Seat

After owning the center of your head so that it serves to bring out the very best in you, you may take a seat—the one that you'll find right at the center of your head where your third eye would be. This is where you will sit to receive the insight of your intuition.

In a moment, you will look for this seat. When you find it, pay attention to how big or small it is, what material it is made of, and what color and texture it is. Is this a seat that has held you before or is it completely new to you? Observe the seat and open up all of your senses so that you can smell it, feel it, and see it in vivid detail. The more time you take now to focus on the seat, the easier it will be for you to access it instantaneously later. Take your time to get to know this seat inside and out, whether you are seeing it, feeling it, or just experiencing it.

Go ahead and sit in the seat in the center of your head. What does this action feel like? What does it feel like beneath you? Are you feeling into the substance of the seat or leaning into its support?

Feel yourself sink into it with all of your being. To me, this often feels like "I am here," "I have arrived," "All is well." For some people, this seat is a recliner, for others it is a throne. Some have described it to be like a control center in the middle of a spaceship, or as if it is a portal to the universe. My seat is a big rock in the center of the ocean, only it is as if the rock is made out of memory foam. It is so comfortable! Yet it also feels solid, sturdy, stable, and reliable—the perfect seat for me. What is the perfect seat for you?

As we have been encouraging you to do, please make this seat uniquely yours, just like everything at the center of your head. Take your time and feel free to try out a new seat each time you visit the center of your head until you experience one that you don't ever want to change. We hope you find this to be your favorite seat in life and that you spend the majority of your time here.

Case Study

Shirin—From Disturbing to Delightful

Shirin felt trapped in an unhealthy situation. The level of corruption at Shirin's office was unbearable to her, but she relied on her job for a work visa and the promise of becoming a naturalized citizen. She knew she couldn't leave the job, at least not yet, but she was miserable. Her body was breaking out into hives, her hair was falling out, she was having nightmares, and she was fast losing faith in humanity. Shirin's boss was especially triggering for her since part of her job was to help conceal his unlawful and unethical actions. Shirin would burst into tears multiple times each week while at work.

Shirin began working from the center of her head. The Center of Your Head tool allowed Shirin to go into work and have the sense that she was the only one in the office, even though she was in the midst of a chaotic work environment. She would put her headphones on and tend to her daily tasks from the center of her head, feeling like she was at a retreat somewhere in the tropics. She said that everyone noticed a profound change in her.

Shirin began experiencing peace and joy regardless of her environment. Coworkers would comment that she was smiling while working and would swear that she must have fallen in love or that she was hiding some secret that was keeping her so peaceful and joyous in a miserable workplace. When she revealed that what had changed in her was the result of her using an intuitive tool, no one believed her. Instead, people started asking her if she was on any medication—not because they were judging her, but because they wanted some. For Shirin, visualization has been more effective than medication.

Shirin's dedication and devotion to the center of her head ultimately increased her frequency so much that she stopped communicating with those same coworkers. It's almost as if she became invisible to drama and chaos. Shirin's clairvoyant healing sessions with me were upgraded from focusing on how to deal with work stressors to improving her personal life, travels, dream projects, and so much more. Shirin changed her life by changing her focus.

Location-Vortex Portal

Technically, this energy tool is a location, a vortex, and a portal. Having a sacred space can be very powerful. This particular sacred space happens to exist within your sixth chakra, your intuition energy vortex. By virtue of it existing here, you are tapped into the answers. By practicing your favorite activity here, you are tapped into the flow of life. Soon your nervous system will recognize this place and respond with total relaxation and harmony. It will feel like a little vacation from your cognitive mind and human form.

Like other tools, the longer you use this, the more real it gets for you. It gains strength, power, and efficacy with each use. The difference between this tool and the others is that you are not constantly creating a new one. It takes you to a reliable location that is unwavering in its service to you.

All you have to do is get to this place and this tool works. It gets easier and easier to get here each time you come back, and before you know it, you will access the feelings and trust that this space promises just by simply thinking about it.

The more frequently you consciously visit this space, the sooner you will have instant access to it no matter what, and no matter where you are on Earth. The center of your head is a location of consciousness. Here you really feel what it means to be the microcosm of the macrocosm, and you are open to the realm of infinite possibilities. See if you can live your whole life from this location—while at work, while in traffic, everywhere. Observe what happens. It is a powerful portal to your truest self.

Congratulations on becoming acquainted with the Center of Your Head tool!

USING THE CENTER OF YOUR HEAD TOOL

Step 1: Concentrate your awareness to the center of your head, between your ears and behind your eyes.

Step 2: Observe the beautiful vista, engaging all of your senses.

Step 3: Look for your highest self, which exists in the center of your head.

Step 4: Have a seat in the center of your head, and tune into your intuition.

Getting Technical on Who Is Doing What

As simple of a place as the center of your head is, for many students, getting it set up can be a little complicated. For the most part, the answer to these technical questions is to choose the visualization that comes most naturally to you and is easiest for you to access. That said, common experiences and questions arise that need some special explanation and guidance.

For example, some students wonder which one of them— their human form or their one- to two-inch highest self seated behind their eyeballs—is the one who receives the Golden Sun, engages the grounding cord, or employs the Separation tool. You might be wondering the same thing. The answer is your human form. Why? Your highest self does not have a grounding cord nor do they need one because charged energies don't exist in the center of your head. If they do, you will ground them out through the trap door that connects with the grounding cord, which is an extension of your larger human energy body. If you are practicing your energy tools from the center of your head, you will be offering your human form these energy tools. Your highest self also doesn't need a Separation tool, only your human form does.

So from the center of your head, from the perspective of your highest self, you will envision a Separation tool that is two feet out in front of you—in front of your human body, and, therefore, also in front of the center of your head. If you are coming from the vantage point of your tiny highest self, this tool could be much, much larger than you. Similarly, you will look down to see a grounding cord around your human hips and it may feel huge relative to how you feel in the center of your head. This is fine! It is also fine if these sizes don't exactly sync up with how things are perceived in the real world. With time you will grow to just accept how things look, and they will become part of the reality of the center of your head.

If you feel like playing around with different perspectives, tune into your whole body from the center of your head. For instance, you could lift an arm and examine it as your highest self in the center of your head—as though you are a tiny being lifting the arm of a human avatar you are operating so you can take a closer look at it. Some of you will have fun with this; for others, it will be more of a distraction and take away from the actual utility of your energy tools.

Many of you will want to keep your focus on your highest self while you are in the center of your head. That is to say, over time, you will begin to lose focus on your physical form and, for the most part, see images in the center of your head through the eyes of your highest self.

This vantage may help you connect more deeply with your highest self and release the biases that come with being human. You may decide to look at people and just experience life more generally through the eyes of your highest self. There's no need to envision that second set of eyes of your human form just beyond the center of your head.

The more you get used to being your highest self, the less you will acknowledge the size and specificities of this location. Just because you are perceiving life from the center of your head, and your highest self may be only one to two inches tall, your Separation tool or other humans will not look huge to you. Rather, you will feel life-sized if not larger than life. Eventually, the center of your head will become a seamless part of your internal landscape, and the line where the center of your head ends and your human body begins will become less and less important to you.

This could take weeks, months, or years. Until then, visualize in a way that feels easy and natural for you. It's more about accessing the energy, neutrality, and sensations the center of your head offers you than it is about getting it technically precise. We are all different, and the center of your head will reflect this difference. It's *your* safe space, so visualize and access it in the way that feels best for you.

*

"Seeing like an anthropologist" derives from and supports the concept of cultural relativism. *Cultural relativism* refers to the notion that humans are, in many ways, products of the social and cultural environments in which they are steeped.

This means that if we were raised in a culture or society different from our own, we would think and understand things quite differently than we currently do.

When anthropologists approach the people they are studying with this understanding, it is much easier to empathize with them, to imagine how it might have been to grow up in their shoes. Generally speaking, when we are able to empathize with others, we are able to recognize the humanity in them, which then makes it easier for us to accept them as they are and to have compassion for them.

If we apply this approach of acceptance to the work we are doing here in this book—perhaps, at first, simply through accepting the images that appear, and over time, accepting ourselves more generally—it will be easier to move on to that next step of developing greater compassion for ourselves, which is a healing in its own right.

Additionally, the Center of Your Head Tool, with which you have learned how to visualize a one- to two-inch version of yourself, helps us develop that empathy, acceptance, and compassion for ourselves, in part because it allows us to look at ourselves from a vantage point that is essentially outside of ourselves. A similar experience can happen when people do visualizations that involve them imagining that they are encountering younger versions of themselves. Imagining ourselves as something separate from us—a projection of sorts—can sometimes make it easier to feel compassion for ourselves, because for many people, the idea of loving oneself can be difficult.

As you continue to see like an anthropologist with the visuals that arise, may your openness to them lead to greater acceptance and love of yourself.

Case Study

Lior—From Submission to Sovereignty

Lior was feeling a loss of autonomy. Lior loved his mother more than anything. When she lost her home in 2008, Lior insisted that she move in with him. He took it upon himself to be her caretaker. She pitied herself, and Lior followed suit and pitied her as well. She would complain of aches and pains, and he would buy her remedies and schedule her healing sessions. She would say she was lonely, and he would cancel his plans in order to take her out and entertain her. Lior became his mother's everything.

At first it started to interfere with his dating life. Then it started affecting his finances. He eventually went from wanting to do everything for her to resenting her for being so needy and dependent on him. Lior realized how invested he had been in his mom's experience and how he was forfeiting his power and his own unique perspective to cater to her story.

Lior discovered that when he remained in the center of his head, he didn't feel sorry for his mother. He didn't feel obliged to drop everything and help her. In fact, he even almost felt envious of her. *Who wouldn't want to live rent free near the beach with a son who adores her?* he thought.

Lior began to regain his independence, and his relationship with his mother changed to friendship. Using the center of his head, Lior was better able to see the situation with neutrality and view his mother as more of a roommate than an obligation. He started asking her to cook him his favorite meals and requested that she google solutions for her problems before coming to him for help.

She felt him pull away a bit, so she started making plans with her friends; she began to come home and tell him all about her adventures. It was empowering for her. The mother and son ultimately regained their friendship and went back to having lovely dinners together, laughing and chatting.

Center of Your Head

While your sixth chakra has always been here, this may be your first time actually residing in the center of your head. Hooray! It's like a point of no return—once you experience this bliss, alignment, and access to your intuition, you will never want to go back.

Allow yourself as much time as you need for the building phase of this tool. Design and redesign it again and again until it's the perfect fit for your serenity, peace, trust, imagination, and intuition. Once you've created it, it will provide you with a safe and supportive space that you can come back to as frequently as you wish. Each return will get more and more instantaneous.

For example, in the beginning you may start by envisioning walls and hearing sounds, and it could take a few minutes to finally take a seat in the center of your head. Before you know it, it will feel like you are teleporting into the center of your head and the experience will be almost instantaneous.

Like maintaining the integrity of anything, the more you tend to the center of your head, the easier it will be to support its power and for it to support you. If you take a little break from being here, it could take you a little while to remember it the next time you visit. The center of your head is such an empowering place. I recommend taking up full-time residence rather than being a tourist.

Chapter Summary

The center of your head is the place to go to access your real authentic self, your intuition, and your imagination. When you are living life from the center of your head, you feel aligned and trusting in the timing of life.

Yay, you! You now know how to dwell in your personal power. You have created a safe, sacred place for yourself through visualization. You have met your highest self, who resides in the center of your head, and you are able to take a seat in the center of your head where you are able to maintain your neutrality. How many people can say all that? You rock!

You can access and utilize the center of your head in four easy steps:

Step 1: Concentrate your awareness to the center of your head, between your ears and behind your eyes.

Step 2: Observe the beautiful vista, engaging all your senses.

Step 3: Look for your highest self, which exists in the center of your head.

Step 4: Have a seat in the center of your head and tune in to your intuition.

Get back into the center of your head whenever you desire an elevated perspective. If you feel overwhelmed by environmental energies, the center of your head will help you see with greater clarity. When you feel crowded out of your own space, head to the center of your head! This is also a great place to go when you want to feel bigger than your problems.

The center of your head is an immediate portal to trust. Come here if you feel triggered. Return here when you feel overly responsible for the experiences of other people. It's also just a nice place to stay a little while. Why not have a seat and simply enjoy the sounds, textures, colors, and sensations this sanctuary has to offer you? Have fun with it, make it your own, and above all, trust that energy follows intention!

SELF-ASSESSMENT

Ask yourself these questions. On a scale of 1 to 5:

_____   *How conflicted am I feeling?* (Where 1 is "My head is spinning; I'm confused, hazy, and foggy," and 5 is "I am clear as can be about my feelings.")

_____   *How much am I trusting the process of life right now?* (Where 1 is "I don't want to trust, I want absolute power and control," and 5 is "It is what it is and it's all working out in divine order whether it feels like it or not.")

_____   *How self-confident are you feeling?* (Where 1 is "I'm full of doubt, often feel imposter syndrome, and am over-critical of myself," and 5 is "I love and accept myself exactly as I am.")

_____   *How empowered is your perspective?* (Where 1 is "Why is everything happening to me?" and 5 is "I see how everything is happening for me.")

PART II
COMMANDING
ENERGY

5
Calling on Spaces to Support You: Grounding Locations Tool

Whether it's to the mosque
Or to the cabaret I go
My aim is always the same
It's to become one with You.
—HAFIZ

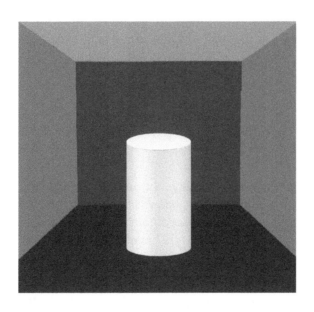

You Belong

We receive so much conflicting information regarding social acceptance—be confident, but not so confident that it's off-putting; self-advocate, but remember to be kind and inclusive in your language; some people will respect you for your high-paying job, but if you spend your hard-earned money like a show-off you may lose their respect. Figuring out how to fit in, gain acceptance, and be your authentic self without ruffling any feathers can be confusing!

I'm going to let you in on a secret: You, my friend, are a unique precious flower, and flowers aren't expected to be anything but themselves. A rose isn't expected to be a peony, just as jasmine isn't expected to be lavender. We also understand that each unique flower species requires a different environment, climate, temperature, and soil concentration to grow, thrive, and bloom.

The Grounding Locations tool will help you plant yourself anywhere you wish and still allow you to thrive and bloom. Using it is like waving a wand over any environment and making it the most supportive one for you—one that offers you the perfect combination of conditions you need to thrive in a way that only you can.

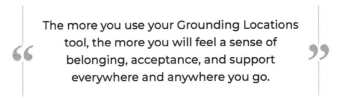

> The more you use your Grounding Locations tool, the more you will feel a sense of belonging, acceptance, and support everywhere and anywhere you go.

When we are in the company of others, some of us empaths have learned to read the room in order to feel safe. If everyone is talking about sports, we can put on our sports cap and do our best to fit in. If we know we're about to enter a baby-obsessed environment, we might prepare to share stories about all the babies in our lives hoping that we will pass the cultural norms testing and be accepted. It can take a lot of guesswork and quite a bit of unacknowledged emotional labor to simply coexist with others in certain environments. Often, all this effort to fit in and belong takes us further away from our most authentic selves.

- Does it feel like your mood, thoughts, personality, and self-expression sometimes change dramatically depending on where you are and who you are with?

- Do you avoid certain social settings because they cause you discomfort? Or if you do attend, do you go straight for the bar to fill yourself up with a little liquid courage before engaging with others?

- Do you find yourself feeling nervous or anxious in new situations or in particular locations or settings?

Your Grounding Locations tool will help your environment support you as you navigate through the various terrains of your day. This tool calibrates the energy field of any location or environment to best affirm and support you. Using it sure is easier than being hyperaware of your surroundings and shapeshifting to match the energy of every location you enter. This simple tool can help you with anything from a first date to a family gathering, from presenting at work to enjoying a night on the town.

GROUNDING LOCATION TOOL AS MEDICINE	GROUNDING LOCATION TOOL AS RITUAL
When you feel out of place	Each day before leaving your home
When you feel invisible or dismissed	Before you enter any new environment
When you are in an environment that doesn't seem to honor your strengths	Before events that require you to be seen—like presentations, auditions, interviews, etc.
If you feel socially anxious and are insecure about the way others receive you	Each time you enter your work environment
In places where you know or feel you are unwanted	Each time you make your bed (You make it once and you can feel great about it all day long, which is much like the way the Grounding Locations Tool works.)
When you are in an environment that feels invalidating	Each time you open a door for the first time that day
In spaces and places that contribute to your feelings of inadequacy	Whenever you put your shoes on (Oh, the places you will go! Let's ground and own them all!)

In just a moment, you will be guided through the steps for the Grounding Locations tool. Before you begin, take a moment to assess how you are feeling right now.

SELF-ASSESSMENT

Ask yourself the following questions. On a scale of 1 to 5:

_____ *How safe do I feel right now?* (Where 1 is "I don't. I don't like it here," and 5 is "I love and accept myself exactly as I am, and know it's safe to be me wherever I am.")

_____ *Am I willing to be seen right now?* (Where 1 is "Nope! I want to hide," and 5 is "I take up space with ease. I feel seen, heard, and understood.")

_____ *Do I feel a sense of belonging?* (Where 1 is "Not exactly. I can't fathom that feeling in this place where I am right now," and 5 is "Are you kidding me? I know I belong and am a valuable contribution to this place.")

_____ *Does it feel like life is supporting your every step?* (Where 1 is "I don't think so. I feel like I'm fumbling in the dark," and 5 is "Yes! I'm feeling the synergy of it all, and it feels like divine alignment.")

Visualizing

By now, you know the drill. Still, remember that practice makes permanent. This time, try to spend a little bit more time focusing on the breath as you begin.

In a moment, you will allow your eyes to close and look within. Start slowing down your breath to begin box breathing as described here.

Inhale for four counts, then hold your breath for four counts, then exhale for four counts, and then hold for four counts. Repeat. Inhale for 4, 3, 2, 1; hold for 4, 3, 2, 1; exhale for 4, 3, 2, 1; hold for 4, 3, 2, 1.

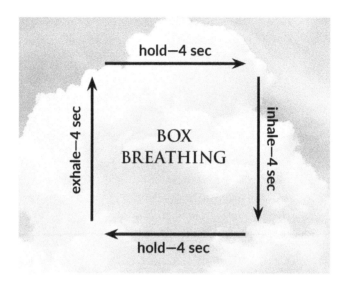

Now, from your mind's eye, imagine the center of the location where you are right now. If you are in a room, imagine that in the center of this room there is a beautiful, beaming, golden column of light. If you are outdoors, imagine it out in front of you at the center of your general surroundings. Just like your grounding cord, this golden column of light is a hollow tube that experiences a gravitational pull within it. In this way, this Grounding Locations tool serves to ground this location, acting as a vacuum and releasing all undesirable energies from this location.

Go ahead and give it a try now.

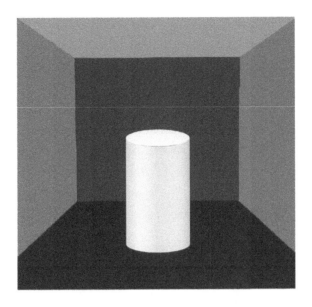

How did it go? Were you able to see it or feel its vacuum?

Technically, the Grounding Locations cord starts at the exact center of the location. It's at the halfway point of height, length, and width. So, if you are in a cube-shaped room that is ten feet high, the Grounding Locations cord would start at five feet high in the very center of the room's length and width. What's most important is that you think of this Grounding Locations cord as having an energetic pull downward and opening up into the center of the Earth.

When you close your eyes again, take a moment to imagine all the dark or dingy colors of this location or room melting off the walls and objects and being absorbed by this bright column of light. Watch as the colors go all the way down the tube and get absorbed by the Earth's center.

If you are outside, you may notice that dingy, murky colors are melting off the natural and built environment and are being sucked into this golden column of light. Watch this location get a little more radiant and shinier as all of this dark and dingy energy gets sucked down this golden column of light and into the center of the Earth.

One of the beautiful things about this tool is that as you are grounding this location, you are providing healing for all life that resides here. From plants to pets to people, all living beings in this location benefit from this golden column of light. As the darker colors are being absorbed—first by this location's column of light, and then by the center of the Earth—you are clearing this space of old, stagnant energy and the thoughts, patterns, associations, and triggers that come with it.

Grounding Locations Remotely

The Grounding Locations tool is especially great when you are preparing for all kinds of highly charged experiences such as auditions, interviews, and meetings. In these cases, you can simply imagine the location from wherever you are currently. If you have never been there before, just give it your best guess and imagine what it will look like. If you have been there before, imagine it in as much detail as possible.

Then, as you engage the tool, imagine it grounding out any limited thoughts, fears, and inadequacies. This will help you avoid vibrating from feelings of insecurity in this space. Because this column of light works as an energetic cleanse for any location, if you would like to release a particular energy in this location, whether it is insecurities, hostility, or judgment, just assign a color to that energy, and then watch as that color is pulled toward and down into the golden column of light.

Just as you did with your own personal grounding cord, go ahead and build a relationship with this Grounding Locations cord. Stretch it out a bit to make it wider and see how that feels. Similarly, you may increase or decrease the pull of the column's vacuum or adjust the thickness of its walls.

Also, by grounding this location, trust that you are reinforcing your own personal grounding cord as well. If you don't ground this space with the Grounding Locations tool, you run the risk of absorbing all the energy that resides there. Luckily, having a grounding cord will help. However, if your grounding cord is the only vacuum in a particular location, that could mean a lot of noisy energy will be running through you, which could be exhausting or confusing. The Grounding Locations tool is a great complement to your grounding cord as they work together.

By offering this location a golden column of light, you are helping heal this entire location and all living beings within it, and you are also allowing your personal grounding cord the opportunity to work for you and you alone, making it much more efficient and impactful.

How's it going? How are you doing with the visuals? Please remember to be gentle with yourself as you become acquainted with this experience. This process is very much like learning and adapting to a new language and culture, which takes time.

You will find that some tools come easier to you than others. This speaks to nothing more than your own unique energy and what is best for you at this particular moment. For example, if one tool feels too complicated or you get stuck every time you try it, take a break and focus on the tools that come more easily to you. It is likely that the ones that come easy are the ones you most need right now.

We are all students here, and my journey with these tools has taken its own unique and circuitous route. Tim and I didn't learn them in this exact order and some were harder for us at first than others.

When I first learned about my grounding cord, I struggled with it quite a bit. No matter how hard I would try, I just couldn't get it to do what I wanted it to do. It wouldn't attach to the ground or the Earth's center; sometimes it would swirl around or even run away from me! It was only after I learned how to work with the Grounding Locations tool that I was able to successfully employ my grounding cord.

I now understand why this was the case: I needed to have the experience of feeling my environment supporting me before I could take steps to ground myself with my grounding cord.

This makes perfect sense! It can be hard for us to be our best and accomplish what we want to do when we don't feel like we belong in the spaces we inhabit. When we feel like we belong, our best selves are able to shine.

Trust that whatever you are feeling and wherever you are on your journey with these tools is exactly where you are supposed to be right now. Just by being here and reading this, you are growing, learning, and aligning with your highest self.

Dogma and Your Practice

These tools can only help you and will not hurt you. Have you ever done a cleanse? Some people will do juice cleanses, others will drink only shakes for a week, some people fast, while others omit specific foods. No matter the type, what commonly happens within the first few days is that people experience headaches or body aches. Some become emotional and others feel lethargic. This isn't because the juices they are drinking are somehow worse for them than the burgers and fries they ate the week before. Rather, it means that the juices of beets and celery may be a bit of a shock to their system because it is not used to them. The headaches, body aches, and other uncomfortable sensations are the effects of their internal homeostasis rapidly adjusting to the new ecosystem. Going from digesting lots of fried foods to digesting only vegetables is a dramatic change, and it will take a fair amount of energy for your body to adjust to this shift quickly. Usually, by day 3 or 4 of a cleanse, all discomfort is gone, and most people feel better than they have in years. Once adjusted, your system can operate efficiently within the new ecosystem. It just takes a little while. People with a relatively clean diet don't often feel the cleansing pains because the internal calibration to the cleanse is minimal and thereby easier on the body.

Applying this same logic, it is easy to understand how, when you first practice the tools, you may experience some "cleansing pains" as your system and homeostasis recalibrates. When I first grounded everyone out of my space I felt terribly lonely. It's not that the grounding cord made me feel lonely—the loneliness was always there, only I did not know it. It took a little while for me to adjust to my new ecosystem, and when I did, I felt peaceful and not lonely. Just like anyone who has ever been on a cleanse, I have become more sensitive to "junk food" or in my case, harboring environmental energy in my space.

What happens when you begin to use these tools is that you become more aware of energy. Sometimes this means you become more sensitive to it. For example, imagine you are in a quiet area completely absorbed in your book and oblivious to anything around you; suddenly, someone points out an annoying buzzing sound in the background, and you lose focus and concentration. You try to get back into your book, but all you hear is that horrible buzzing sound! Had it not been pointed out to you, you never would have noticed it, but just because you hadn't noticed it before does not mean it did not exist.

You certainly don't have to ground every location you ever enter, and even if you forget to set up a Grounding Locations tool for a place that you intend to, it is fine. You have made it thus far without them, so there is no harm in skipping them. However, because you are aware of their influence and impact, you will be more sensitive to them now.

You will notice when locations are grounded and when they are not. This doesn't mean it is harmful when they are not grounded; it just means that you will notice whether they are or are not in a way that you didn't before. Now that you have this tool, you will likely acquire a preference for it, and so stepping into an ungrounded location may make you feel as if something is a little off. The good news is that all of these tools can be practiced preventatively as rituals or in the moment as medicine. And the more you practice, the more you will be able to offer them to yourself on the fly as needed. If you notice that you have stepped into an ungrounded place, simply take a moment to ground it, and just like that, all systems will be recalibrated, and you will have set yourself up for maximum support and flow.

A closet, bathroom, or other quiet space can double as a meditation hall for those of us that have a hard time multitasking and using these tools while doing something else such as making conversation or tying your shoe. Just get yourself to a space where you can take a moment to get your tools all set up. You might just feel like a superhero changing into their uniform. Boom! Costume change, and now you are a supernatural force to be reckoned with!

Now close your eyes again and do your best to observe the Grounding Locations tool in as much detail as possible.

USING THE GROUNDING LOCATIONS TOOL

Step 1: Locate the center of the location you would like to ground.

Step 2: Create a golden column of light in the center of this location to ground it.

Step 3: Imagine any dark, dingy colors and disserving energies leaving this location and going down the golden column of light.

Step 4: Own the location by imagining your name and image on all the walls.

Case Study

Daniel—From Predictability to Possibility

Daniel did not understand why his wife insisted on spending so much time with her parents when all they would do is bicker and complain. After visiting her parents, he and his wife would always find themselves in a bad mood. For Daniel, it was all just a big waste of time, and he could not help but resent spending his days off this way.

Daniel would moan and groan and huff and puff before they got to his in-laws. He would begrudgingly put on his Peace Mediator hat for them even though what he really wanted was some peace for himself. And then he would complain about what an awful time he had the entire drive back. His wife would get defensive, so the two of them would essentially argue about her parents' arguing on their drives to and from their house. His wife didn't think the bickering was that bad, and she would tell Daniel he was too sensitive and that it was he who had the problem, not her parents.

When he first learned about the Grounding Locations tool, Daniel was skeptical and had difficulty believing it could actually have an impact. Every visit had been exactly the same for years, so he had little faith that an energy tool could change that.

The first weekend he applied the Grounding Locations tool to his in-laws' property, his father in-law spent the whole visit talking with their neighbors about a problem with the fence between their properties. Daniel took this as an opportunity to turn on the TV and watch the big game he was expecting to miss that day. It was glorious! When the fence talk was over, the neighbor came inside and sat alongside Daniel. They bonded over the game. He now had a buddy in the house, *and* he was able to do one of his favorite things in the very location he had historically dreaded. Was the tool working? "No, it's just a coincidence," Daniel insisted to himself.

Still, he tried it again on the following visit, certain it would be yet another boring, bickering, frustrating day at the in-laws. He was partly right. This week the bickering was back, but something had shifted. Daniel found himself being entertained by his in-laws rather than taking them so seriously. As he watched, he found them to be quite comical. He allowed his wife to do all the talking for a change and just sat back and enjoyed the scene.

He didn't know he was capable of simply observing and was thrilled to discover this. He was also imagining colors going down the Grounding Locations cord, which served as a productive distraction from the actual conversations at hand. This practice also offered Daniel a sense of power and control he had not experienced there before. It was official, the Grounding Locations tool would become his magic trick for these visits.

Ultimately this tool changed Daniel's relationship with his in-laws. He felt more at home in their place without pressuring himself to interact with them too much. They noticed a change in him, and it was almost as though they became even more dramatic and performative for him. As far as he could tell, their bickering had turned into their little comedy bit, and now it all felt like an inside joke that only he was in on instead of a problem he felt put out by or felt responsible to resolve.

This work has a ripple effect. Without all that commotion bookending the visits, and since Daniel resigned from his role as mediator during the visits, his wife was no longer reacting to him. Without her focusing on Daniel's displeasure of being there, her parents' bickering took center stage, and she started to better understand where he was coming from. Ultimately, it helped her better understand his years of advocacy and protesting. She saw these visits in a new light. She even thanked him for reluctantly coming along with her all these years, recognizing how noble he had been.

Owning Locations

Now that you have started to become familiar with your Grounding Locations tool, let's take this a step further by owning this location. You now know that grounding a location benefits *all* life within that space. Owning a location is like setting its dial to tune into your unique energy frequency so you can experience a sense of belonging and purpose there. Whether it's your home, your office, a restaurant, a stage, a place you have never been, or one that you frequent, owning a location makes you that much more comfortable and confident there. Owning a location illuminates all the reasons why this location is on your path and how it is helping you actualize your purpose.

Your Name

Imagine your name written on all of the walls of your current location. If you are outdoors and there are no walls, imagine your name hanging on the trees, or etched into another physical object or landmark there. Matter holds onto energy, so writing your name in the matter of this location is like declaring this location as your partner on your evolutionary path. Once you own a location, you will notice it is easier to be there. You will feel more supported.

What form your name takes is entirely up to you. You may own this location by hanging huge neon signs of your name everywhere. Or perhaps you would prefer your signature on all the walls. Maybe today you would like your name in print or big block letters. However you choose to display your name, take a look around and notice it beaming back at you from every edge and corner. You belong here. This space is here to support you.

Your Image

Just as you did with your name, you may want to hang an image of yourself throughout this location as another way of owning it. Your image could look like a painting of you, or it could be a polaroid, a headshot, a cartoon, or some other depiction of your likeness. Whatever feels best is best. As you take an intuitive look all around you, you see yourself shining and smiling back at you. This place is now tuned into you so that it may offer you the maximum amount of acceptance and affirmation. What matters is that you like what you see on the walls, and that it helps you feel more like yourself and more comfortable in that location.

Creating images on command is new to most people, so most of my students begin by imagining stick figures or sketch drawings. If you have a favorite photo of yourself that you have committed to memory, visualizing that could be an easy way to start using this tool. As your visualization muscle strengthens, the images you conjure will become more detailed.

If you identify more as a younger version of yourself, then it's perfectly okay to use that image. It works best if you do see yourself in the image you pick. If an image of the way you would like to look one day inspires you, then it's okay to use that instead. I would be mindful of this one, however. If you see yourself in that image, it may help you materialize that version of yourself. But if that image of yourself feels unattainable and far away, it may work against you and leave you feeling even less supported by that space.

For example, let's say you want to gain twenty pounds. You envision hanging up an image of yourself at your goal weight. For some, this will work as intention-setting, kind of like a vision board. Seeing that image over and over again will feel great, inspiring, and electric. Every time they are in that space, they will feel light, proud, and great about themselves. For others, however, this image may feel like torture. It could inspire feelings of shame, judgment, and disapproval—feelings that are generally unhelpful and unproductive when someone is attempting to own a space.

What is most important is that whatever depiction of yourself you choose to hang on the walls helps you to feel connected, grounded, heard, seen, and understood. Whether that's you at age five, you after five in the evening, or you with an extra five pounds.

You can own a space by either writing your name on the walls or placing your image on the walls. Either is perfect, and if you would like to do both, that works, too! Whether it's your name, image, or both, you now have the signage to use when owning locations. Just like with all the tools, make it yours. Create the perfect ambiance for you to feel like you belong here.

*

From an anthropological perspective, the power of owning locations is clear. Often when people don't readily have power in a society, they seek ways to have power and demonstrate their power to others. Being recognized as powerful by others essentially makes a person powerful, whether because of their socioeconomic status; their privileges that come with being part of the dominant race, gender, or ethnicity; or because they wear the clothes, drive the car, and speak the language and lingo of those with power. Social scientists often refer to this as *status*.

Another way of achieving power/status among one's community is by symbolically claiming physical spaces as one's own. Think about a parade that celebrates the ethnic heritage of a particular group of people. Police block off streets and cars wait in traffic jams to allow groups of people to parade through cities honoring their cultural traditions. We see this in Brazilian Carnival and New Orleans' jazz funerals—those who often don't have the most power in society are temporarily given the opportunity to not only take up space but also to take up space that is not normally considered theirs.

Similarly, anthropologists and sociologists have argued that graffiti, sometimes quite literally writing one's name on a location, is a way of owning it, and this is more likely to occur among people who do not experience a clear sense of ownership and power in the society or community in which they live.

Of late, we have seen a proliferation of painted murals decorating cities worldwide. Interestingly, in Tim's city, an artist has begun to hang enormous canvas portraits of individual people—many of whom come from minority communities—on buildings throughout downtown.

When we are able to see images of ourselves, or even people who look like us in our environment, we are more likely to feel a sense of belonging.

Go ahead and own the locations that you want to support you, and know you are participating in a long-held tradition that speaks to the human need for belonging.

     You belong here.

Owning Shared Spaces

Whenever I teach this tool in person, I have anywhere from twenty to two hundred students simultaneously owning a room. And you know what? Every individual feels a greater sense of belonging after this meditation. It is not a competition. Multiple people can and often do own a location at the same time. This makes it so everyone wins, and all relationships within the location may be mutually beneficial.

As a concert-goer, if you own the location, you are helping yourself receive the perfect concert *for you*. This may mean you are deeply moved emotionally, or you have a clear view of the stage, or maybe it means you feel the synergy and connection in the space. Each concert goer can have a completely different experience, all while owning the same location. This tool will cater to any location to serve your spiritual needs. Similarly, when the performers own the concert hall, they are setting themselves up for a performance that benefits them as it is pleasing the crowd.

When everyone in the room grounds and owns the room, it fosters greater communication for all. There is plenty of space for all living beings in any location to own that same location. In fact, if all of us did own locations, we would probably have less competition and fewer power struggles and more synergy and collaboration.

 When we all feel that sense of comfort, support, and belonging, it is easier for everyone to self-express.

Since grounding and owning locations is so validating, it becomes easier to hold space for others to express themselves, as their expression is not a threat to your own existence or significance.

If you are in a space with others and you are the only one owning it, others will likely default to you as the leader of the vibration there. They may not even be aware that they are doing this. Imagine the lead singer of a band being the only one owning the concert hall. The other band members may feel resentful or like they are living in the shadow of that one person. If all the band members owned the concert hall, however, they would be affirmed in exactly why they are there; this would help each of them feel valued, significant, important, and impactful. Owning a location helps you be the main character of your life story without having to be the lead singer.

When I was in grad school, one of my classmates had a really hard time with her shift supervisor—the person responsible for overseeing students' interactions with their patients. My classmate had a very delicate and meek energy about her, which contrasted greatly with the bold and brazen nature of her supervisor. She swore the supervisor didn't like her. She felt uncomfortable throughout her shifts and wished she could be more aggressive like her supervisor, but that could not have been farther from her truth.

When I taught my classmate this Grounding Locations tool, she grounded and owned the clinic space every day leading up to her next shift. When it was time for her clinic shift, she entered the space feeling more confident and was able to focus on her patients rather than her supervisor. She called me immediately after her shift to report the news—this particular supervisor, who was known for being stingy with words of praise, concluded the shift by applauding my classmate on her stellar job! Her supervisor literally clapped for her, as did her classmates! Everyone was surprised, as this gesture was completely out of character for the supervisor.

"This really works!" she exclaimed through giggles and bewilderment when I next saw her. "I mean, I didn't think my supervisor was even capable of such a thing! Can you believe she praised me?" Of course I could. I had been practicing this tool for years and knew exactly how powerful it was. In this example, the entire work shift was set up to reinforce my classmate's energy, as she was the only one that grounded and owned the space. Her actions hadn't changed at all, but the vibration dominating the room that day had changed entirely.

The tool had been working even before she received praise. The praise was just an added bonus. When you change your energy field, you change your life.

Case Study

Michele—
From Martyr to Matriarch

Michele felt invisible and taken for granted. For as long as she could remember, all Michele had ever wanted was to be a mother. So when she married and had three kids, all of her dreams were coming true. However, after a while, Michele would look around her supposedly happy home confused as to why she felt so overwhelmed and insignificant much of the time. She loved her family but also felt like she was losing herself to them and fading into the background. She described herself as a house elf. It was as if she was so good at anticipating the needs of others that they almost never acknowledged her.

For Michele, it was not enough to have a huge grounding cord in the center of her home. Although this was the home she always wanted, it no longer felt like hers. She decided to go through her home and offer each space its own grounding cord and set a different intention for each of them. She set the pantry to hold and contain, while she calibrated the kitchen to nurture and nourish. She set the dining room for connection and collaboration and the living room for entertainment and relaxation. She loved organizing her energy field in this way and took great joy in making this a daily morning practice. After the kids were off to school, she would walk throughout her home, replace all the grounding cords, and reset each intention.

When Michele started grounding and owning her home, she felt a renewed sense of power—she was the queen of her castle. She began to look around her happy home and feel pride rather than overwhelm and confusion. She was better able to see all the items and systems in place that were a reflection of her unique frequency. She now knew that this home was more *her* home than it was anyone else's, and now she could actually feel it!

Michele went from feeling invisible to feeling like a strong matriarch. She went from merely living in the home to ruling it, which caused her to take her role more seriously than before. The Grounding Locations tool gave Michele her power back and reminded her of all her many blessings that had been there the entire time!

Intention Setting

When you are grounding or owning a location, you can simultaneously set an intention for your time there. Writing your intention on all the walls makes it that much easier for you to live in alignment with it. If the location is where you will have an audition or interview, your intention may be for it to reflect your pure potential. If the location is your office, perhaps you would like your intention to be clear communication, synergy, or joy. Your intention can be one word or a short phrase. Whatever your intention is for the specific location where you are right now, imagine writing that intention out. When setting an intention, it is best to keep it in present tense. For example, choose a phrase like "I feel heard," rather than "I will feel heard." Take a look around and notice your name, face, and intention(s) beaming right back at you.

Sometimes working with these tools can surprise us. Tim has a great example of a time when he used the Grounding

Locations tool and didn't get a job that he interviewed for. This does not mean the tool didn't work. He believes it worked quite well, just not in the way he had expected.

Early in Tim's academic career, he was invited to interview for a position at a university in the Pacific Northwest. He was stoked! Yet no matter how beautiful he thought this region of the country was, he hadn't ever envisioned living there. Before he knew it, he was being flown out and wined and dined by his potential future employer.

I remember that before he left home, he engaged his Grounding Locations tool. Because he hadn't been to this exact location before, he did his best to imagine the room where he would be interviewed and give his job talk to faculty and students. When he grounded these locations remotely, he also owned them by imagining writing his name and hanging a photo of himself on all of the walls. He also set the intention for this location to bring out his full potential.

He told me that as the plane descended over the Cascades, he was suddenly enchanted with the landscape. Though he had driven through the region a few times on road trips, he had never flown there before, so this perspective was new and felt amazing. This feeling set the tone for the remainder of his trip.

In one-on-one conversations with students, faculty, and staff, he felt confident to be himself—professional, friendly, and open, all at the same time. The interview process with the committee was a fun intellectual chat with like-minded colleagues about all kinds of topics they were interested in discussing with him. As you might imagine, the job talk was similar. He felt empowered and in his element there, talking about his research and entertaining interesting questions from the audience. By the end of the interviewing experience, he felt great, and was confident that it couldn't have gone better.

On the last day of the trip, it was unusually sunny and warm—especially for February. Tim had plans to see an old friend who he hadn't seen in years who lived in the area. Not long after she picked him up, he received notice from his airline that his flight had been canceled due to a Nor'easter back home, and he wouldn't be able to get on a return flight for three days!

The subsequent days were some of the warmest and sunniest February days that locals had experienced in years. Tim's friend invited him to stay with her family, and while his home back East was buried in snow, he relished in it all, taking in the scenery and falling in love with the area.

In the end, as I mentioned, Tim did not end up getting the job. As he thinks back on that experience, he knows with so much clarity that landing that job was not the point of that trip. It was about the experience of being recognized for his work and feeling like he belonged in a place that he came to love. Also, as a person who now knows he needs a decent amount of sun in his life, he does not believe it was a coincidence that his time spent there was unusually sunny. He felt wholly supported by the location, and he looks back fondly on that experience as a positive contribution to his career path and self-confidence as an academic.

Intentions Compared to Goals

Intentions are when you are aligning your personal energy with a feeling that reflects your value system. *Intentions* are an experience rooted in the present tense, whereas *goals* are future oriented. Goals are often measurable outcomes we can plan for and strategize around. Differently, intentions are lived each day, independent of achieving the goal.

If you are calling in romantic love, the intention could simply be "Love," or even "The feeling of security that a relationship offers," whereas a goal would be something like "Be in a committed partnership." It is best to leave other people's karma out of your intentions, so, instead of writing, "I have a life partner," or something similar, a more appropriate intention would be, "I feel loved."

That said, I personally believe writing an intention such as "I am in a healthy relationship" is okay and can even be beneficial if you are using it as an intention and not as a goal. If you are using that sentence to access the feeling of a healthy relationship as a way of calling one into your life, that is an intention. On the other hand, if you are using that sentence as a goal, it could draw your focus to what you don't have and lead to you feeling unfulfilled, inadequate, or like a failure if you don't establish such a relationship.

Intentions leave us open to the realm of infinite possibilities. Intentions are limitless and expansive. They are focused on effort and not outcome. In contrast, goals are generally limited to an outcome and can leave us feeling contracted and small. When goals are specific, they can narrow our field of vision and thus, our ability to receive or recognize affirming miracles coming our way.

Had my classmate set a goal to be recognized by her shift supervisor, it would have been really disappointing if she hadn't been recognized that day. Instead, she kept the focus on herself and set the intention to feeling confident in the clinic, nothing more. That is all it took, and that is all she really cared about. The praise from the supervisor only reinforced her confidence, but she was feeling confident before the praise. The praise reflected back to her that the tool was working! But her feelings of confidence were all the affirmation she needed. As a result, she stopped dreading those shifts. Similarly, in the story about Tim earlier, had Tim set the goal of "getting the job," then he may have been disappointed by that trip, which was clearly not the case.

Intentions help you feel inspired and motivated with a sense of purpose and alignment with your greatest potential. They help you expand your perspective in current time and space and are not focused on the future. They are a daily practice, not a strategy.

Case Study

Abdul—From Scary Space to Sacred Space

Abdul had performance anxiety. Abdul was in finance and worked on Wall Street. He had recently gotten a promotion, which entailed greater responsibilities, one of which involved a weekly presentation. Each week it was the same. Abdul would have insomnia the night before the presentation, feel nauseous the whole day leading up to it, and be on the verge of a panic attack during it. He dreaded it so much that he was almost resentful of his promotion. This environment was cutthroat, and he much preferred fading into the background.

Abdul knew the presentations would take place in the same conference room every week. He started grounding and owning that conference room every day, and he would write his name on all the walls and set intentions such as "deep breaths," "eye contact," and "I feel impactful." By the time Abdul had to give his next presentation, he had calibrated the space to intentions and his delivery, and his confidence and anxiety improved with each passing week. He was energetically aligning with the space daily just for that experience that took up one hour each week. Using the Grounding Locations tool minimized the experience. It became routine as it was something he visited daily.

Each time he used the Grounding Locations tool in that space and each time he hung up an image of himself on those walls, it was like adding an extra coat of paint so that the walls became more vibrant and denser. He was painting the walls his favorite color so the space was no longer a corporate conference room—it was now Abdul's personal stage.

Using the Grounding Locations tool daily had a cumulative effect so that Abdul's relationship with the room grew stronger and more beneficial each time. The tool helped Abdul build a new association with speaking and presenting. That conference room shifted from a scary space to a sacred space. Abdul now teaches this tool to all his new hires.

Increased Efficacy

You will remember that grounding cords lose efficacy with usage. The same goes for the golden columns of light in a location. If you continue to use the same Grounding Locations tool, it will sit there as a tube of old energy for a little while until it ultimately fades and decomposes with time. A good habit to get into is replacing your Grounding Locations tool frequently so the location is current and clear of energetic debris.

The length of time that a golden column of light lasts depends more on the location it is in rather than the number of days it has existed there. Destroying a column of light is like raking leaves. If you don't rake them, the wind will carry them elsewhere; they will naturally decompose and disappear with time. Yet it is far more efficient to rake them up and put them where you want them. If you are in a place with many trees shedding leaves, you will want to rake them daily, whereas if you are in a location with one small tree that hardly sheds, you could get away with raking much less often. Similarly, if you are in a highly charged environment, we recommend that you destroy and create a new Grounding Locations tools daily—sometimes hourly—but if you are in a more neutral environment, you can probably go a lot longer before the energetic debris starts to build up on the walls of the column. Just know that you can never overdo it. There is no harm in frequently destroying your old Grounding Locations tool and creating a new one.

Your Grounding Locations Tool

Tim and I both love this tool because of its simplicity. It is always a golden column of light. It is always in the center of the room. You always own a room by seeing your name or image or both on all the walls, and if you like, you can always use the same signage over and over again. Intention setting is completely optional. The simplicity and repetitive nature of this tool makes it easy to create a habit in grounding and owning locations. It also makes it easy to apply this tool to any location big or small, near or far, indoors or outdoors. No matter the space, you will go through the same motions.

Like all the energy tools you have learned thus far, your Grounding Locations tool is both a healing tool and a diagnostic tool. You will notice some places take longer to ground than others as there is a lot to release. You will walk into other places and notice you already feel like you own them before you even hang your signage on all the walls. Because we don't tend to take locations as personally as we do other tools in this book, this tool invokes less self-talk, biases, internal conflict, or self-deprecating thoughts.

I remember when I first learned about my Golden Sun, I was constantly judging myself; it was too small or I was not filling it up entirely. When I started using my grounding cord, it took me a really long time to get it directly beneath me and even longer to get it to stay attached. I was resisting grounding myself, and then I was really hard on myself for this resistance, and I layered feelings of defeat, judgment, frustration, and more into the process. Inevitably this made it harder for me to ground in the first place and gave me more work to do and more energy to ground out once I finally did get my grounding cord to stay. This Grounding Locations tool doesn't seem to invoke the same kind of thoughts, feelings, or self-dialogue so integrating and implementing it comes more quickly and naturally for most. We don't take this tool personally because it's not personal.

The other thing about using this Grounding Locations tool is that you are superimposing your golden column of light and your signage onto matter. You are using your imagination in conjunction with the material, visible world. It's like the visualization process has started for you and you just have to complete it. Someone started the painting, and so the focus and direction are already built into the process. You are not left with that responsibility, which saves you a lot of effort. You can always practice this one with your eyes open if that's easier for you. Simply imagine the golden column of light in the center of the room where you are now. You can even use this tool in a room where pictures of you are already hanging on the walls so you won't even have to produce those; all you have to do is recognize the pictures. Easy peasy!

Chapter Summary

Your Grounding Locations tool will help you feel supported and affirmed in any environment, foreign or familiar. Use this tool to call in support from any location. Ground spaces with a golden column of light for greater synergy and flow for all. Own spaces by hanging up signage that represents you for increased confidence and connection to your purpose everywhere you go. Should you wish to set an intention for a space, be certain it's an intention and not a goal so it may bring out the best in you and offer you an opportunity to rise to that vibration.

You can set up and implement your Grounding Locations tool in four easy steps:

Step 1: Locate the center of the location you would like to ground.

Step 2: Create a golden column of light in the center of this location to ground it.

Step 3: Imagine any dark, dingy colors and dis-serving energies leaving this location and going down the golden column of light.

Step 4: Own the location by imagining your name and image on all the walls.

The Grounding Locations tool is most useful in moments when you enter a new location or place that makes you feel uncomfortable. Call on this tool when you are feeling a lack of power or if you would like to experience a sense of belonging. This tool is also helpful in preventing the energy of others from influencing your mood or thoughts. Your Grounding Locations tool will help you feel calm and confident in a particular space and can be especially helpful when you would like to make a great first impression, whether it's in an interview, for an audition, or on a date. Use this tool as an ally in historically charged environments like family gatherings, holiday parties, or work meetings.

 Walk your path with purpose, grounding and owning each location along the way.

May all the spaces you inhabit serve your greater purpose and may you recognize what a gift you are to any location. As with all the tools, please make this one your own! Have fun with the design and sizing of the signage. Take note of how you feel before and after using your Grounding Locations tool. Explore this tool with particularly charged spaces or events.

SELF-ASSESSMENT

Ask yourself the following questions. On a scale of 1 to 5:

_____   *How safe do I feel right now?* (Where 1 is "I don't. I don't like it here," and 5 is "I love and accept myself exactly as I am, and know it's safe to be me wherever I am.")

_____   *Am I willing to be seen right now?* (Where 1 is "Nope! I want to hide," and 5 is "I take up space with ease. I feel seen, heard, and understood.")

_____   *Do I feel a sense of belonging?* (Where 1 is "Not exactly. I can't fathom that feeling in this place where I am right now," and 5 is "Are you kidding me? I know I belong and am a valuable contribution to this place.")

_____   *Does it feel like life is supporting your every step?* (Where 1 is "I don't think so. I feel like I'm fumbling in the dark," and 5 is "Yes! I'm feeling the synergy of it all, and it feels like divine alignment.")

6

Working with the Laws of Nature: Creation/Destruction Tool

The Beloved—Source of suffering
and Remedy for suffering.
—HAFIZ

Flow With It

This book meets you at the intersection of free will and destiny. How so? *Free will* suggests you have all the power in your life, and you can manifest anything you wish! *Destiny* implies that what is for you won't pass you by and that certain experiences are fated, whether you desire them or not.

Your Creation/Destruction tool helps you tune in to the currents of life so you are able to go with the flow (destiny) in an empowering way. You will *create* this tool to remember the powerful badass you are (free will), and you will *destroy* this tool to make room for magick, chance, and opportunity.

Commanding energy in this way will help you flow and not force. This tool will help keep you in the power seat in a humbling and accepting way.

We learn in science class that energy is neither created nor destroyed. For something to come together, something else has to break apart. It is a natural law, but it is one that is not mirrored back to us in the current age. We don't farm like we used to, so we are disconnected from recognizing the nature of creation and growth in this very real way. We live in a world focused on productivity and all we create. We celebrate our creations and often mourn destruction as if it is a bad thing. Destruction is not good or bad; it is natural and vital to creation. Creation cannot exist without destruction.

I was born to be a spiritual teacher and acupuncturist. I know this because the moment I surrendered to my path, it was as if the clouds had parted, and life has grown easier with time. I now know it's my destiny; however, as I mentioned in the introduction, due to the conditioning and messaging I grew up with, I struggled to allow myself to dream this big and had convinced myself I was meant to be a dentist.

After I began using my Grounding Cord tool, I came to understand how much of my past I was bringing into my present. It was clear I needed to let go of it all! I asked myself *Does the current me even want to be a dentist?* With my Creation/Destruction tool, I accepted that I am not alone on this planet and my life will always be susceptible to outside energetic variables. I dropped the illusion of believing that I was in complete control of my life. Instead, I adopted the position that I am in complete control of my actions and my responses.

The Creation/Destruction tool helps you focus on your efforts and all the places your power is. For most, the more empowered you feel, the easier it is to adjust to disappointments or unwanted experiences. If you recognize yourself as a powerful creator, then destruction won't feel threatening to you because you know you can always create again.

This tool is equally helpful in the art of letting go. You will go on to destroy every balloon you create. So you don't have the opportunity to get too attached to the outcome of your efforts, you will place the emphasis on your efforts and not on outcome. You will focus on your path, not a destination. The destruction part of the tool helps you realize that destruction is a part of life, that destruction is inevitable and not always personal.

After months of using this tool while I was taking classes to pursue a career path that didn't spark my joy, I started going with the flow of my life. I realized how miserable I was as a dental assistant and as a student studying science. My best friend during my time as an undergraduate often suggested I become an acupuncturist, which used to irritate me. However, once I began using this Creation/Destruction tool, I felt more expansive and liberated to actually hear that suggestion. As a result, I gave it a shot and applied to acupuncture school just out of curiosity. I hadn't really thought through what I would do if I got accepted, but I was more open to the possibility of not being a dentist than ever before. I attribute this to all the time I was spending each day destroying and letting go of attachment with my Creation/Destruction tool!

To my surprise, I got accepted into acupuncture school! I am sure that without this tool, I never would have applied in the first place, and even on the off chance that I had, I never would have been able to trust the energetic flow of my path without this tool. I would most definitely have forced a dental career onto myself. After all, I am a strong believer in free will, hard work, and devotion. I know I could be a dentist right now out of sheer will; I also know how unfulfilled, unexpressed, and out of alignment with my highest self I would have been had I forced that path into existence.

May this tool set you free to be who you were born to be and help you apply your free will to elevate your destiny! Ask yourself these questions:

- Does it feel like you are stuck in a rut? Or like life is on autopilot, and you are going through the motions but lack connection and fulfillment in all you do?

- Are there times when you feel like you are forcing a boulder up a hill or swimming against the current?

- Do you often take setbacks, redirection, or course-correction personally, as though you have done something wrong?

Your Creation/Destruction tool will help you recognize that you are the commander of your vessel as you traverse the ebbs and flows of life. You'll realize that while you may have some big, beautiful ideas about your life, perhaps there's something even bigger and better out there for you. You will build trust both in yourself and in the process of life so you feel like you are in partnership with life's natural cycles. You will grow and glow with greater flexibility and confidence.

CREATION/DESTRUCTION TOOL AS MEDICINE	CREATION/DESTRUCTION TOOL AS RITUAL
When you are not getting what you want and it's starting to feel personal	Any time an object breaks (Honor the destruction energy and go with the flow.)
When you feel like life is an uphill battle	Before engaging in a new hobby (For example, before you sit down to paint, use this tool to cocreate with energy.)
When you have forgotten where your power is and how to access it	Before engaging in a new habit, like reading before bed or having a juice in the morning
When you need to alchemize anger into movement	Each time you throw out an object, appliance, or item of clothing that is no longer serving its function
When you are feeling stuck or are breaking through old habits.	With each new object you invite into your life
When you are deriving your self-worth or identity from external sources	With each new opportunity you invite into your life

In just a moment, you will be guided through the steps for the Destruction/Creation tool. Before you begin, take a moment to assess how you are feeling right now.

Visualizing

Here we are again! By now, you are a pro.

In a moment, you will allow your eyes to close and look within. Start slowing down your breath to begin box breathing as described here.

Inhale for four counts, then hold your breath for four counts, then exhale for four counts, and then hold for four counts. Repeat. Inhale for 4, 3, 2, 1; hold for 4, 3, 2, 1; exhale for 4, 3, 2, 1; hold for 4, 3, 2, 1.

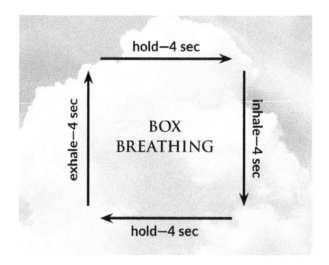

Creating the Balloon

Begin by envisioning a red balloon two feet in front of you. Look at this balloon. What shade of red is it? What size and shape is it? Are there any shiny parts to it? Spin your balloon around and create and observe it from all angles. That's it! You are really visualizing a red balloon! Wonderful! Please take a moment to acknowledge what a powerful creator you are.

Go ahead and take another moment to admire your work. Take in this red balloon. You may spin it around or flip it over or simply stare at it as it is for a bit. Again, notice its color, texture, and contour.

Destroying the Balloon

Next, you are going to pop this red balloon. It's as simple as watching it explode into a million pieces until it disappears completely. If it's helpful, visualize bringing in a needle or sharp object to pop your balloon.

If you haven't already, take a moment to close your eyes and give it a try.

So? How did it go?

Were you able to feel the release? When it pops, all that energy that was contained in the balloon is being released back out into the universe. By destroying your balloon, you are releasing any of your own energy that was contained in or attached to that balloon. By doing this, you are subconsciously accepting the idea of impermanence and relinquishing a bit of control. Brilliant work!

The Creation/Destruction tool was the first of the tools that I taught Tim; he practiced with it for a couple years before learning the other tools. At the time, Tim was getting his PhD and was so focused on his writing that he was prone to obsessing and overthinking. Like most PhD students, he felt insecure about his ability to complete the degree and about his professional future more generally, which only caused him to desire control and to tighten his grip on things.

I recommended that he create and pop balloons almost daily. To help establish a practice of it, he established a ritual: He would do it while sitting in front of a little altar in his bedroom. He also took full ownership of the tool by adding his own little take on it. "I would close my eyes and ask the universe to help me decide what the balloon should look like. It was different every time—bright blue, translucent with glitter, orange and elongated, etc. In doing so, I was already cocreating with the universe and trusting that whatever appeared was the right balloon for me at that specific moment in time," Tim explained.

In just a bit you will learn how to allow your balloon to absorb energy that you want to release so that you can then destroy it. Tim added another dimension to this process. Because the energy that he wanted to release was coming from him, he had the impulse to blow air out of his mouth as he envisioned the energy leaving his space and being absorbed by the balloon. This added to the ritual because now he had the sensation and sound effect of air coming out of his mouth.

Because Tim had already developed some sound effects, he went ahead and added another detail: He made the sound of an explosion the moment he popped the balloon. No joke! It may sound a little bit like child's play, but it made the tool a little more fun for him. It helped him not take himself too seriously while it simultaneously helped him visualize the balloon breaking into a million little bits.

Bottom line: Have fun with these tools! They are here for you, and the more you recognize that, the better they will work.

Case Study

Andrés—From Infatuation to Emancipation

Andrés was falling in love, and it was all he could think about. His thoughts had become obsessive in nature. He was in his early fifties, and this was the first time in his life that he had met someone he could imagine settling down with. This new relationship was so unexpected that he couldn't get it out of his head. He found himself spending an inordinate amount of time daydreaming about his new girlfriend—all the adventures they would take one day, all the sex and cuddling they would experience, even the home they would eventually build together.

Andrés's attention span for everything else seemed to dwindle by the day, and he was on the verge of becoming a disaster at work. He could barely stay focused during important meetings as his mind would keep drifting back to this new, incredible person in his life. A couple coworkers noticed that Andrés seemed distracted and brought it to his attention. This made Andrés realize that he needed to get his daydreaming under control.

By using the Creation/Destruction tool, Andrés was able to put all of his thoughts and emotions in one place: a love balloon! He believed creating and destroying this balloon would help him regain his focus and accomplish the tasks at hand. Creating the balloon seemed to be the impactful part for Andrés. The enormity of his feelings felt insurmountable and uncontainable. He felt like they would take over his heart, mind, and life, and since he loved the sensation so much, he wanted it to stay forever.

When he was able to see all that love, lust, and admiration contained in one rather large balloon, he felt that he had sovereignty over his mind and thoughts again. Seeing this huge balloon outside of himself made him feel proud of the love that he had called into his life, and it helped him recognize that he could conjure this feeling or balloon up any time he needed a hit. Creating these balloons helped Andrés trust that the love was his to keep and that it would last even in the absence of the balloons or his obsession.

Destroying the balloons helped him release obsessive thoughts that were rooted in fear and scarcity. After a few days of popping balloons, he realized the reason he had been so resistant to releasing this energy was because he hadn't trusted that it would last. At first, he thought each balloon he popped might be his last. But it only took one week for him to realize he had an infinite amount of love to supply to endless balloons! He also recognized that after popping balloons, his love for his girlfriend remained strong; he was just less obsessed, which helped him start recognizing the difference between the two.

Andrés had a blast with the balloons! In fact, he taught his girlfriend about them, and they would both use them when they were triggered or obsessed. They realized that without the balloon energy in their space, the relationship grew in a more peaceful and grounded manner. The love grew even while the obsession faded. In addition, Andrés's relationship with the obsession changed. Any time he would start to become obsessive, he would acknowledge the instinct with a warm smile, and then invoke the tool in a snap. Andrés now has it all: the career, the romance, and the mental freedom!

＊

Let's get back to it! Now you will create a blue balloon. Look two feet out in front of you and create a beautiful blue balloon. Take a moment to visualize this balloon with as much precision and detail as possible. What shade of blue is it?

What shape and size is your balloon? Can you see the knot in the rubber at the bottom of the balloon?

Give the balloon a twirl and take it all in.

Filling the Balloon with Energy

This time, watch as you fill the blue balloon up with any blue energy in your space. Let's assign a value to that energy that you will be releasing and destroying. Let's assign all the color blue in your space to sadness energy. Great!

Now, watch as all the blue you see in your space leaves you and enters your balloon. Imagine all this blue energy entering your balloon, blowing it up, bigger and bigger.

Take your time to get all the blue out of your space and into the balloon. You may wish to focus on the balloon inflating and growing with your blue or you may prefer to watch the blue leave you. You may even be able to witness both happening at the same time.

Even if you are having difficulty visualizing any of this, as with all of this work, trust that it is happening because you are intending it to happen. So, whichever way you experience it, let all the blue go. Once you have released all your blue into the balloon, it's time to pop and destroy it.

Watch as your blue balloon explodes into a million pieces that all disappear completely. When this happens, the universe is taking back all this liberated energy and making great use of it as you are breaking patterns, habits, and associations with sadness. When you detach from your creation and any attachments that you have created for yourself associated with your creation, you experience a sense of relief. Now take a moment to scan your body and simply take note of wherever you feel the most relief.

As mentioned earlier, the Creation/Destruction tool was the very first of these tools that Tim ever learned. At the beginning, he remembers thinking that he definitely wanted to feel the relief that comes with destroying the balloon, but maybe he was just psyching himself into thinking that he was actually feeling it. He was really grappling with the difference between wanting to experience something and actually experiencing it.

I reminded him just how powerful desire can be. If you want to feel something enough, that desire can align you with the feeling. It's kind of like "fake it until you make it," which is rooted in behavioral psychology, and can truly work. "Energy flows where intention goes" really resonates here.

Relatedly, imagination and intuition are only a frequency apart, and the difference between desiring and actualizing is irrelevant when it comes to these tools. With enough practice, you will build a habit, and actualizing the balloon and filling it up with energy will replace your desire to do so. Until then, you may experience more desire or a combination of both. It could be more imagination than intuition, but because they are so energetically similar and create almost the same result, the difference between the two is irrelevant. This has absolutely been my experience with visualizing all of these tools.

Practice will help you differentiate as well as actualize and intuit with confidence. Desire and imagination will fuel your practice and are part of the journey. You will soon discover that the two are not as different as you think. They are more interdependent than they are independent of each other. One doesn't cancel out the other. Rather, imagining and intuiting reinforce each other.

You will find Creation/Destruction tools to be most useful when you can't get your mind off something, when you are feeling overly attached to a particular outcome, or when you are feeling any kind of stuck. Basically, whenever you want to shift energy in order to be better aligned with your highest self, pull out this Creation/Destruction tool.

 Create and destroy to set yourself free and be who you were born to be.

Every time I start destroying things in my life unconsciously, I turn to this tool. For example, when I begin to notice things breaking or shorting out more often than normal—small things, like coffee mugs and lightbulbs—I know it is time for the Creation/Destruction tool. Sometimes when I fall out of the habit of implementing this tool, larger things in my life begin to malfunction—glitches with my website, invoices not being processed, or larger things falling apart around the house, like plumbing, intercom systems, doors, and so on. Yet the moment I start popping balloons—creating and destroying with intentionality and consistency—all of the destruction seems to cease around me and wonderful creations begin to pour in! I often think about how helpful it would have been for me to know about this tool when I was younger. I probably could have avoided at least a few of my car accidents!

Case Study

LaRhonda—From Attitude to Gratitude

LaRhonda was very ambitious and a high achiever. She was also impatient. Things were never moving fast enough for LaRhonda. She felt like she was always waiting on something or someone. It was a real challenge for her to work with others, and it became increasingly challenging for others to be in her company. Her impatience often resulted in her being overly judgmental about virtually anything in her life.

After getting into some heated arguments with a few different longtime friends, and after another friend called her out, La Rhonda suddenly became aware of her impatience, her self-righteousness, and her obsession with control. But even with this newfound awareness, LaRhonda was stuck. She couldn't seem to stop herself from becoming irritated with nearly everyone around her.

LaRhonda felt dejected. She knew what her problem was but couldn't seem to solve it. The more she recognized her impatience and self-righteousness, the less impatient and forgiving she became with *herself*.

LaRhonda learned the Creation/Destruction tool. She started popping balloons every time she found herself becoming impatient. She would put all of her judgments into a balloon and explode it. She would put all her feelings into a balloon and make it explode. She would imagine the colors leaving her body and inflating the balloon, and then she would pop it. LaRhonda warmed up to the tool quite quickly. In fact, she had so much fun with it that she began to see these moments of impatience as opportunities to get a fresh perspective and to feel better.

As a result, LaRhonda found herself meditating quite a bit throughout the day and enjoying it. This tool ultimately offered her patience, which benefitted all of her relationships and her overall outlook on life.

Breaking Patterns

Let's create another balloon to help us break patterns, release the ego, and get back to spirit. Think of a habit you engage in that you would like to let go of but are having a hard time releasing. Perhaps you want to quit smoking cigarettes or you would like to let go of negative self-talk. Maybe you want to stop dating people that don't help you feel valued. You might want to take a few moments to think of an unwanted pattern. Take your time.

Okay! Ready to break free?

Imagine a yellow balloon two feet in front of you in as much detail as possible. As you do, remember you are bigger than your patterns and circumstances. In creating this yellow balloon, you are recognizing yourself as a cocreator with the universe. You are aligning yourself with your power. Look at its particular shade of yellow, the evenness or unevenness of its surface texture, its size, and its shape. Twirl this yellow balloon around to fully take it in. Great work! You are creating with such ease! You are so powerful!

Imagine that any yellow in your space represents the habit or pattern that you have decided to discontinue. Scan your space for the color yellow and command all of the yellow to leave you and your energetic space and fill up the balloon. Watch and feel all the yellow leaving your body. Notice how it fills up the yellow balloon. The balloon is growing and expanding with all of your yellow energy. Keep it going, removing all the yellow from your space.

Once all of the yellow is in your balloon, go ahead and pop it, destroying all that the color yellow represents for you. Watch as this balloon explodes, is absorbed by the universe, and disappears completely. The universe will make much greater use of all this energy. By creating it, you are taking ownership of this balloon and the energy it absorbs. By destroying it, you are acknowledging that as powerful as you are, other energies will always affect you. It's just part of the human experience. We are all in this together!

You are allowing yourself a new way to be and are even making room for a new identity to come along with it if you so choose. You are taking a courageous step forward in the name of personal growth and evolution. You are ascending. Way to go!

USING THE CREATION/DESTRUCTION TOOL

Now take a moment to close your eyes and practice visualizing the steps of the Creation/Destruction tool on your own.

Step 1: From your mind's eye create a balloon about two feet in front of you.

Step 2: See this balloon in as much detail as possible.

Step 3: Have this balloon absorb any unwanted energy from your space. The energy could be the same color as the balloon.

Step 4: Send this balloon far away from you and pop it to destroy it until it disappears completely.

Case Study

Stella—From Breaking the Law to Breaking Free

Stella was in an arranged marriage. Her husband had chosen her, but she had not chosen him. She never wanted the marriage but didn't have much of a say in it. She felt trapped. Her husband was a good person, and he smothered her with gifts, attention, and anything her heart desired, so she felt guilty for not loving him back or wanting to be in the marriage, which didn't help her mental health.

Even though he showered her with the finest things in life, she grew to resent all her beautiful things because they were not what she actually wanted. The items felt like golden handcuffs.

One day while Stella was shopping, something came over her and she intentionally left the department store without paying for an item she wanted. What a rush! She didn't know why she loved the experience so much—was she hoping to get caught? Was jail more inviting than her home? Did she perhaps want something of her own that wouldn't show up on her husband's credit card statements?

After the rush settled, Stella felt terrible. She knows theft is wrong, and she could certainly afford the item. To make things right with the universe, she decided to donate it.

Sixteen years later, Stella had become a professional shoplifter. She did it on a near daily basis. It was the only sense of power and control she had in her daily life. She looked forward to doing it and loved getting away with it. Nevertheless, each time, a few hours after the event, guilt and self-loathing would inevitably set in, which only perpetuated the pattern. Stella was now not only trapped in her marriage, she felt trapped by her own mind and body as well. Shoplifting had become a compulsion that left her feeling powerless.

Stella started using the Creation/Destruction tool. She popped balloons almost non-stop as her urge to shoplift was almost constant. She especially popped balloons whenever she wanted to walk out of a store without paying. Sometimes it worked, and she would put the item down. Other times, she would walk out and feel the high, which felt like an old familiar friend that she enjoyed. When the remorse would settle in, she would visualize that energy, direct it into balloons, and pop one after another until she felt lighter. For some time, she popped *a lot* of balloons each day, even each hour. The balloons helped Stella before, during, and after the trigger.

Because the balloon popping helped Stella avoid the downward shame spiral after shoplifting, her cravings reduced in intensity. Therefore, she didn't yearn for a rush if she wasn't feeling a heavy low. She used this tool to forgive herself and set herself free from both the shame spiral and the thrill-seeking habit.

Through much conviction and devotion, Stella broke her shoplifting habit! The high she experienced from breaking free surpassed any shoplifting high that she had ever experienced by far. She hadn't believed she could stop until the pattern ended.

Although Stella began popping balloons to destroy one limiting behavior, it worked to subconsciously remove all limiting behaviors in her life. Soon after kicking her shoplifting habit, she filed for a divorce. Stella had become empowered and broke free of all the invisible chains that were binding her.

About Your Frequency

This work has both a shelf life and a cumulative effect. The shelf life suggests that the effects only last for so long. Popping one balloon likely won't break a long-standing habit. However, popping a balloon every time you feel the itch just might! The more you do it, the stronger this muscle gets, and the easier it is to do it again and again. That is the cumulative effect of this work.

The more frequently you practice these tools, the deeper the work goes and the longer the results last until they become incorporated into your new approach to life and your destiny. Once using these tools becomes a habit, the essence of them is more internalized, and you can reduce the frequency with which you practice them. For example, if you are only popping balloons once each week, it is kind of like going back to square one each time you do it. Whereas if you are popping balloons daily, you are continually reinforcing this muscle, which grows stronger with time. The results last longer with time too!

Another rule of thumb is that the longer you have had the pattern, the longer it will generally take to break it or quit it. If you have been smoking for only a week, then twenty minutes of popping balloons in one sitting might just do the trick. However, if you have been smoking for twenty years, you will need to pop a good number of balloons, and it may take weeks, months, or even years for you to break the cycle.

Of course, the results also depend on the person. Some chronic smokers may instantaneously quit after just twenty minutes of balloon popping, while someone else who has been smoking for only one week may require months of popping balloons. The results will vary, just like individuals vary.

＊

As you now know, the Creation/Destruction tool is great for when we have strong attachment to outcomes. That's great right? But wait, what about the power of positive thinking? How about the power of visualizing the life you desire? So which is it?

Tim and I both remember having these thoughts when we first learned about this tool. The following chapter introduces you to the Manifestation tool, and there we will go deep into explaining how it works and how it can benefit you. In the meantime, let us explain what we have learned from this work: The answer is "both and." It can be highly effective to visualize in order to manifest what you want, *and* it is also just as important to not become overly attached to that which you desire to manifest.

Let's say you are interested in buying a home, and you have a very clear image of what you want in your head. You can visualize every bit of it—the color of the door, the layout of the house, even the landscaping! There is absolutely nothing counterproductive in visualizing this way. The trick is letting go of that image after asking the universe to provide it to you. This is an essential part of manifesting that lots of people don't know about or practice. Believe it or not, if you become too attached to this very specific image of your ideal home, you might actually end up sabotaging yourself and not acquiring the ideal home due to too much attachment to the image of it.

Becoming too narrowly focused on the details of something that you want can cause you to not see the forest for the trees. You may have come across that very house only with a different colored door, and you may have overlooked it just because it did not perfectly match your image. If you had remained open to multiple timelines and versions of what you desired—in different packaging or even at different timing than you had hoped for—you would have been able to see that your home was right beneath your nose.

With too much attachment, we slip into our ego mindset, suggesting that we are in this all by ourselves and that we don't require the help of the universe. Detaching from attachment and outcome aligns us with the spirit and purpose of the manifestation, allowing us to cocreate with the universe.

So, when you become too attached to how a person, place, or thing should appear or be experienced, you may unintentionally prevent yourself from receiving them. Such instances are perfect for engaging your Creation/Destruction tool.

Your Creation/Destruction Tool

Some people use this tool as an alternative to the Grounding Cord tool, whereas others love using it when they become angry, frustrated, or find themselves in a rut. After you practice creating and destroying for a while, take some time to think about how you relate to the process and when you like to use it most.

Also consider if you are more of a creator or a destroyer. Take note of what part of this tool comes more naturally to you. Is it the conjuring of the balloons I enjoy or is it their destruction? When I destroy them, do my balloons disappear fully or does it take a while before I am able to release all of the little tiny pieces to the universe? What's my relationship like with this tool? Do I enjoy the creation? Am I kind to myself as I am bringing up images on command? Do I feel a little bad or guilty when destroying? Does the destruction offer me a sense of relief or freedom?

Every day somewhere between 60 and 84 billion of our cells die. If you think that is a lot, how about the fact that we create something like 330 billion new cells each day? Where I am going with this is that life and death are two sides of the same coin. We cannot have one without the other. The same goes for creation and destruction. Now when things fall apart I'm confident that even better things are coming together. Now each time I lose my wallet, keys, or sunglasses (a monthly occurrence, ha ha), I actually get excited about all the new I'm calling in!

I'll never forget the year I ended contact with a community that I used to hold very dear to my heart. I felt blindsided by the events that led to breaking ties and was heartbroken. A week later, however, I attended a birthday party where the only person I knew was the guest of honor. Wow, the difference in the dynamics between this person's friendship circle and what used to be mine was like night and day. The conversation was elevated and stimulating, these people were so self-realized and proud of one another's accomplishments. They were altruistic, positive, and so much more my vibe. I was so inspired by every one of them and a few of them are among my closest friends. I entered that party mourning all that was destroyed and left the party celebrating this beautiful community that I was now a part of. Destruction often proceeds creation.

Our world tends to glorify births, gains, and productivity while shying away from discussing loss and death. As a collective, we are not entirely seeing reality as it is, which can create internal conflict. May your new Creation/Destruction tool offer you peace by helping you become more aware of what is and is not serving you. May it help you set yourself free from a limited perspective so you may accept yourself and your life unconditionally.

Chapter Summary

The Creation/Destruction tool is a great one for those struggling with impermanence. Change is the only constant, and your Creation/Destruction tool will help you gracefully shift with many of life's changes. Evolution is the ability to adapt to a changing world. Think of your Creation/Destruction tool as an evolution booster so you can go from growing and evolving to expanding and ascending.

This tool will help get you out of tunnel vision so you may see things from a different perspective. If you are feeling like a dog with a bone or if there is something in your life that you just cannot drop, pop some balloons! Seriously, pop many, many, many balloons. It helps! You will likely shift from cyclical thinking or obsessive thoughts to a more elevated perspective and flexible mindset.

The first part of the tool—creating the balloon—reminds you of all you *do* have control over and just how powerful you truly are! The second part of the tool—destroying the balloon—reminds you of all you do not have control over and helps you let go with grace. By intentionally creating and destroying, you are tuning into the nature of your cycles and working harmoniously with yourself and with the universe.

You can exercise your Creation/Destruction tool in four easy steps:

Step 1: From your mind's eye, create a balloon about two feet in front of you.

Step 2: See this balloon in as much detail as possible.

Step 3: Have this balloon absorb any unwanted energy from your space. The energy could be the same color as the balloon.

Step 4: Send this balloon far away from you and pop it to destroy it until it disappears completely.

Remember, if you find yourself unconsciously destroying (breaking things, bumping into things, or losing things), devote a little extra time to this tool. Regular use will help reduce and resolve disappointment. If it feels like you have been stuck in a prolonged era of destruction, rest assured, an equal amount of creation will soon follow—it almost always does! Just keep going, popping a variety of balloons along your way.

 You are nature becoming aware of itself. Change your approach to life, and your life will change. Embrace the shift.

SELF-ASSESSMENT

Ask yourself the following questions. On a scale of 1 to 5:

_____   *How flexible and accepting am I feeling right now?* (Where 1 is "Everything is wrong. I cannot accept this," and 5 is "I'm bigger than my situation, so there's nothing I can't accept. I'm a mind yogi.")

_____   *Am I recognizing my power right now?* (Where 1 is "I have no power here," and 5 is "Yep, it's all about attitude, not altitude.")

_____   *Am I sensitive to rejection?* (Where 1 is "Yeah, of course. I take rejection very personally. It hurts!" and 5 is "Rejection is protection and sometimes divine intervention and redirection. I'm grateful for it.")

_____   *Do I trust in the process of life?* (Where 1 is "No. I haven't had that privilege," and 5 is "Yes! I trust it's all working out for my highest good, even if I don't understand how just yet.")

7

Creating the Life You Desire: Manifestation Tool

Let us pour wine into a punch bowl
Hurl roses into the air
Crack the ceiling of the heavens
And cast a new design.
—HAFIZ

Visualize to Materialize

This is easily every student's favorite tool. Why wouldn't it be? Euphoria, awe, wonder, play, inspiration, and imagination are the key ingredients to your Manifestation tool. We have already laid the foundation for this tool by discussing the difference between goals and intentions when we introduced the Grounding Locations tool. Now, we will distinguish between achieving goals and manifesting dreams. A major difference between the two is that manifesting dreams is a spiritual act that comes from the heart and requires feelings and emotional alignment, whereas achieving goals is an intellectual act that relies on your mind, strategy, logic, and, oftentimes, grit. Whereas goals may motivate, manifestations will inspire.

Look at all you have created for yourself through your rational mind. It's pretty impressive, I'm sure! Now, imagine all you can create from your intuitive mind! It's a sacred gift that transcends the limitations of logic so you may live a limitless life!

One of my favorite manifestations happened while I was skydiving. As we were ascending to the jump-off spot in the sky, my instructor asked me if I wanted to do anything specific on the descent—perhaps flips, zigzags, or maybe I would like to land on the beach? I said that I have always wanted to kiss a cloud. I asked if maybe we could jump through one. He looked at me sadly and said, "It's a really clear day. There are no clouds for you to jump through. I'm so sorry."

Right then I closed my eyes for a few seconds and utilized my Manifestation tool. Keep in mind that I had been using this tool for over a decade, so I could access it and execute it at lightning speed. I imagined a single cloud in the sky, and I watched, felt, and experienced myself jumping through it. I was delighted by the sensation. A few seconds later, I opened my eyes, surrendered the manifestation, and joined the conversation the others in the plane were having, not giving my manifestation another thought.

By the time we jumped, I was so overstimulated, nervous, and giddy that I completely forgot about wanting to jump through a cloud. Suddenly, my instructor spotted a cloud, and we both got super excited! We zoomed toward it, and as we got closer, we were able to see a circular rainbow right in the center of the cloud! Seriously. Not only did I manifest jumping through a cloud, I got to jump through a rainbow!

The rainbow in the center of the cloud was a greater manifestation than I could have ever imagined! Often when manifesting, something even better than your desires comes through. Manifesting is expansive, and the practice will expand your mind and your capacity to receive and hold miracles. It may inspire so much rapid growth within you that by the time your manifestation actualizes, you will have outgrown parts of it that you once desired.

 May this tool inspire you to rise to the frequency of your deepest desires!

Use your Manifestation tool to actualize anything you wish. The greatest gift to come from this tool is the personal transformation process that comes included with this practice. Can you relate to any of these questions?

- Do you feel like you are settling or playing small in some areas of your life?

- Are there times when you feel that great things only happen to other people?

- Would you like to achieve your goals without having to rely solely on self-motivation, willpower, and drive?

- Do you believe that with more money come more problems?

Your Manifestation tool will help you recognize that life is not happening to you but rather for you. You can use this tool to call in experiences big or small. There is a reason you want what you want. By manifesting, you will connect with that reason so that all you manifest is a reflection of your self-worth, reinforcing your purpose here on Earth.

MANIFESTATION TOOL AS MEDICINE	MANIFESTATION TOOL AS RITUAL
When you are feeling pessimistic, uninspired, or depressed	Every Spring Equinox when nature is focusing on new beginnings
When you feel envious of what someone else has	Every new moon
When you feel powerless or hopeless	Every birthday, as a way of celebrating yourself
When the gap between where you are and where you want to be is causing you pain	When considering new major purchases
When you feel invisible, small, overlooked, taken for granted, or like an afterthought	Before searching for a new employee, employer, or service provider
When you are clear on what you desire but uncertain of how you will actualize it	With each new relationship, experience, event, or opportunity you are considering inviting into your life

In just a moment, you will be guided through the steps for your Manifestation tool. Before you begin, take a moment to assess how you are feeling right now.

SELF-ASSESSMENT

Ask yourself the following questions. On a scale of 1 to 5:

_____   *How magnetic and deserving am I feeling right now?* (Where 1 is "More like unworthy and cursed. I never get what I want," and 5 is "I feel like the luckiest person alive sometimes! All my wishes are coming true!")

_____   *What is my relationship with desire?* (Where 1 is "Ugh. I hate it. It tortures me," and 5 is "I've embraced desire as a part of life and find it adds value to my life. Desire brings out the best in me.")

_____   *What would I do if all my dreams abruptly came true?* (Where 1 is "Gosh, that sounds a little intimidating and anxiety-provoking. I don't know what I would do," and 5 is "Eeeeeee! I would celebrate, naturally! I would integrate them all into my life with so much gratitude.")

_____   *Do I feel worthy of everything I want?* (Where 1 is "Nope. I feel inadequate and sometimes experience shame" and 5 is "Are you kidding me? I was born for this!")

Visualizing

Now that you have begun building your visualization muscle, let's apply it to the most sensory-oriented visualization of them all!

In a moment, you will allow your eyes to close and look within. Start slowing down your breath to begin box breathing as described here.

Inhale for four counts, then hold your breath for four counts, then exhale for four counts, and then hold for four counts. Repeat. Inhale for 4, 3, 2, 1; hold for 4, 3, 2, 1; exhale for 4, 3, 2, 1; hold for 4, 3, 2, 1.

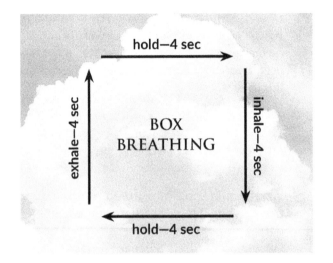

Setting the Scene

Before you dive into conjuring the exact thing that you would like to bring into your life—whether it is an object, an experience, or a sensation—begin by painting the scene and fully engaging your senses so that you are powerfully present to receive just what you are asking for.

Where will you be when this manifestation actualizes? What do your surroundings look like? Are you indoors or outdoors? What can you see in the foreground? What is going on in the background? Are other people present? Do you notice any familiar landmarks, vegetation, or other objects, such as artwork? What colors are capturing your eyes? What time of day is it?

It's fine if you don't have the exact location figured out yet. Just trust yourself and focus on the feelings and sensations that come up as they are most important. I ask students to conjure up details, like the specific location of their manifestation, only to reinforce the feeling of actualizing it, so if you can get to the feeling without such details, go for it!

As you continue with this tool, you will start to realize how productive it is to have fun and play when you are using it. You will also come to see how what you are manifesting is a reflection and an extension of you. Whether it's the job, home, relationship, or whatever else you wish, this tool is all about learning *why* this is the perfect manifestation for you and *how* this manifestation brings out the best in you. The job doesn't define you; you define the job. The home doesn't define you; you define the home. Similarly, you are the manifestor, so be mindful not to play victim to whatever it is that you are calling in. You deserve it! You are worth it! And there's so much more to you than this one thing. Just like with all relationships, a little bit of flexibility and compromise benefits everyone.

Case Study

Ruth and Emilie— From Cold to Connected

In addition to being her best friend, Ruth is Emilie's mother. They often had deep philosophical conversations that were both enlightening and hilarious. And when they decided to turn some of their spiritual inside jokes into a fashion brand, it became a hit! The apparel line gained momentum far more rapidly than they had ever expected.

What started off as a bonding passion project was now a thriving business, and with this newfound success, came a new focus. They were so excited about all the sales that they had called in "by accident," they were eager to see what they could call in on purpose.

They now had growth strategies, self-imposed deadlines, employees, and more responsibilities. They were stressed. After working together all day, their quality time diminished and their personal relationship suffered. The playful spirit that had started the business was gone. Now it was all spreadsheets and sales calls. They lost focus of the process, the joy, and the soul of the business. It went from passion to prison, and they went from besties to colleagues.

They were devastated by this and couldn't see a way out of the loop. They had different visions for the business, and both felt unheard by the other and a general loss of control. They agreed that because the business had cost them their relationship, it owed them. The least they could do is maximize their profits—as though any amount of money would be worth losing such a beautiful and rare connection.

It would be of highest service for Ruth and Emilie to realign with gratitude and desire. Their business was a product of their intuitive mind, right? And now their rational mind had taken over and was kind of holding them both hostage.

The energy tool that could best help them through this hiccup was abundantly clear: the Manifestation tool. They practiced this tool mindfully. Knowing they were both in a pessimistic place, they took a very long time to set the scene before diving into the actual manifestation. It also took some time before their breathing patterns changed and they felt like they were ready to visualize accepting and receiving their manifestation, which involved reconnecting with their bestie, prioritizing their relationship over their business, and realigning with the passion and purpose of their business.

During the meditation, tears went streaming down their faces. At one point Emilie almost reached out to hug Ruth. Their hearts were expanding and their mindset was shifting. They returned to the love and abundance of their situation. They took a moment to connect with the power of their love and take pride in the legacy they had built with so much joy and amusement.

After they came out of the meditation, they held each other for a while. They had missed each other so much. They both now realized that they had foregone necessary self-care while their business was growing rapidly so they decided to close up shop for a week to have a spa moment and reconnect.

Life was going better than ever. Ruth and Emilie now recognize the importance of connection and play in their relationship and in their business. They have been practicing their Manifestation tool monthly ever since as a way to keep their growth rooted in passion and purpose. They learned where to place their focus—the playful nature of their priceless bond—and where to relinquish control and how to trust the ease of their growth.

Remember that we are constantly cocreating with the universe. In other words, you are not doing this work alone in a vacuum, and therefore, you will be able to actualize this experience when there is synchronicity and spiritual significance for all parties involved. That means we need to consider quite a few different karmic paths, so please do not get too fixated on any one particular location or variable in your manifestation; holding on too tightly to such specificity could mean you miss out on the spiritual purpose of this experience, as Tim pointed out earlier when we were discussing the Creation/Destruction tool.

※

Now let's return to the manifesting. Continue to take in whatever sensations come up. What does it sound like here? Is there any background noise that you are able to decipher? Try your best to get a 360-degree view of this space and take it all in, noticing all that you are seeing and hearing.

What does this place feel like? What is the temperature? How does the air feel on your skin? What about any smells? Can you distinguish between any scents? Fragrant flowers? The scent of your beloved beside you? Your favorite incense? A delicious meal cooking in the background?

Take a moment to fill in any blank spots in your surroundings. Fill them in with whatever you wish, whether it is more color, vegetation, or other objects. Take it all in. You are right here, right now, residing in the moment where your manifestation actualizes.

No matter how deep we get into this work, the sensorial experience of our human selves is still activated while we are visualizing. By this we mean that we continue to receive stimuli, whether we hear noises, feel the air, or smell scents in our surroundings.

As you build this imagery muscle, your attention to those sounds, smells, and feelings will fade into the background, and you will be better able to pay attention to what you are imagining. When this happens, you will be better able to call in sensations that are more relevant to your manifestation.

For now, we would characterize those external sensations in your immediate surroundings as interference energy. This interference is common with this work, even if you have been doing it for a long time.

You can ground this energy out with your grounding cord or just not pay it any mind. The less you focus on these external stimuli, the less of a distraction they will be. Rest assured, these sensations will not compromise your manifestation in any way. They are mere distractions, nothing more.

Energy flows where intention goes, so redirect your energy to your internal world. In doing so, you will fuel it with power and realize that you are bigger than your situation. On the other hand, if you continue to pay attention to your outside world, you will give your power away to it, telling the universe that your situation is bigger than you.

If you continue to have difficulty tuning out those unwanted stimuli, simply incorporate them into your manifestation and then layer your own sounds and smells on top of them. The point is to keep focusing on what you are creating and conjuring and to be proud of yourself for doing this work!

As with all of the tools, this will get easier with time.

Witnessing Yourself Receive

Now let's zoom in on you. Take a moment to observe yourself in this scene. Are you sitting, standing, or moving? What are you wearing? What accessories are you donning? How does your posture and body language look? Take in this future version of yourself with as much detail as possible, accepting whatever comes up.

And now, without further ado, it's manifestation time! Go ahead and visualize that future version of yourself receiving the exact thing you have been wanting to manifest whether you are watching yourself win a competition, pick up your new car, or actualize inner peace.

As you witness yourself receiving, observe how this manifestation affects you. How do you react to this dream coming true? Are you overcome with happiness, are you screaming and squealing? Are you dancing? Are you crying? Are you jumping for joy? Perhaps you are in awe and have become completely still.

Relish in this moment. Feel all the excitement and enthusiasm it has to offer you. Celebrate all that you are calling in. Acknowledge yourself for creating this manifestation in your life and allowing it to happen.

How exactly are you celebrating your dreams coming true? Can you feel the endorphins flooding your body? Can you feel your serotonin bursting through the roof? Are you laughing? Are you silent? Are you celebrating and receiving alone or is someone there with you? Whatever comes up, hold onto these feelings.

Now, take a moment to recognize all the ways this manifestation is benefiting you. How is it improving your quality of life and adding value to it? Give thanks for all that is! Think about all the ways this manifestation is serving you and the ripple effects of all those ways.

Perhaps you manifested a new car that is safe and rides smoothly, and so the result is that you arrive at work in a wonderful mood, which helps you see the stress of work in a different light. Or maybe you are so joyous over this car that you can't stop smiling all day, so it boosts the morale of your entire office.

Think of all the ways this actualization is improving upon what already is. You so deserve this! You are completely worth it!

Detachment from Desire

Now, begin to give thanks for all you already have. This will help you detach from this single manifestation. As lovely and helpful as this manifestation is, it is equally important to remember that you are tremendously blessed with or without it.

When you detach from your desires, you avoid enduring unnecessary pain and suffering. By practicing detachment, you declare to the universe that your desires are an extension of you. They exist because you exist. You are the creator. Conversely, when you are too attached to your desires, you tell the universe that your desires are bigger than you, which can lead to you feeling like a victim to them.

In order to manifest, it is crucial that you accept that just by being you, you are absolutely worthy. And whatever it is that you are calling in is a reflection of your bright light, and not the other way around. Giving thanks for all you are and currently have aligns you with that understanding.

Take a moment to feel the depth of gratitude you have for all that is in your current life—possessions, relationships, or accomplishments. Give thanks for your bed, food, friends, the clouds in the sky, the trees on your street, your lungs, your liver, and every single one of your internal organs. You have so much to be grateful for! Counting your blessings will help you feel blessed and empowered; you can keep perspective and not become desperate to manifest your desires.

✳

One of my favorite parts of this tool is witnessing myself get so excited about receiving what I have long desired.

However, it is entirely possible that you may see yourself being unimpressed by one of your manifestations. If this occurs, we would encourage you to treat this as an opportunity to learn about yourself.

For example, maybe the journey *was* more important than the destination for you. Maybe it wasn't so important for you to get the thing as it was for you to have the experience of working to achieve it. In pursuit of this particular manifestation, perhaps you have already ascended to its vibration and even surpassed it.

Maybe the manifestation represented something you felt was out of reach, and by the time it materializes, you feel so completely worthy of it that it is not as exciting anymore or it is no longer as much of a leap to imagine it as yours.

Another reason you may be unimpressed in your visualization is that you are trying protecting yourself. Perhaps you are so attached to a particular outcome that you have given your power to it and know you would feel devastated if you didn't achieve it. As a result, you do not allow yourself to get excited because you are afraid of being disappointed. We can relate to this as both of us grew up in families that warned us not to get "prematurely excited" about attaining things, as if doing so would jinx the process. We recommend trusting in our respective highest selves on this and just going with what feels best for you.

 You are worthy, just by being you.

Releasing Sabotaging Energy

Now, if you zoom out a bit, you can visualize containing this entire manifestation in a bubble that is hovering a few feet in front of you. Concentrate on the bottom right area of the bubble, and you will notice a cork. Release that cork and let all the self-sabotage energy in the bubble drain out with ease and grace.

We all carry some of this energy around with us, and this step of the visualization works to acknowledge, honor, and heal that energy. Watch as this self-sabotaging energy drains out of the bubble. It may look like water, sand, or tar. Simply observe its release until it has drained out completely. Once it has, place the cork back into the bubble.

Accepting, Receiving, and Blessing

Now you will check in with a gauge that reads how willing you are to accept and receive this manifestation. It's a gauge that reads from 0 percent to 100 percent. Checking in with your gauge is helpful in cultivating self-awareness and learning a bit more about yourself.

Imagine bringing up a gauge on the outside of your manifestation bubble. Your gauge may look like a circular odometer or like a linear thermometer. I like to use a rainbow that reads 0 percent on one end and 100 percent on the other. Whatever you choose for a gauge, set it up now, and ask it to reveal to you how willing you are to accept and receive this manifestation. Trust whatever percentage it lands on. If it's not already at 100 percent, then set the gauge to 100 percent. You so deserve this. You are worthy of actualizing this experience!

Early on, the needle on my gauge would be all over the place, and it would be moving back and forth. I used to super glue it to 100 percent and then tie it down and anchor it with a padlock. I did not trust the gauge to stay at 100 percent. I did not trust that I was worthy. Plenty of times my gauge would move back and forth and not settle on a number. In hindsight, I see how I did not have the self-love or courage to receive that feedback, so I saw no feedback at all. These tools are really something! They do get you into the experience of life and out of your head.

Like most people, your analytical muscle is likely over-developed and your intuitive muscle is underdeveloped. This is normal, common, reinforced, and rewarded in Western culture. We are taught to judge, examine, and overthink. We are taught to look before we leap and to think before we speak. This book is asking you to set that training aside.

At first your body will fight putting your rational mind on the back burner, and doing so will feel counterintuitive. This is just your mind doing its best to keep you safe in the best way it knows how. My mind was interpreting the number on that gauge as my destiny and forgetting entirely that I have free will here. Trust that you are not a victim to that number; you have all the power to change it, should you wish to. The more you self-explore and own your power, the more you will grow to appreciate that number and the easier it will be to read.

Back in my disordered eating days, I would dread stepping on a scale. The scale determined my mood and worth, or so I believed. Trust me, I'm much heavier these days than I was then, but I love myself way more now! The scale no longer scares me; it offers me helpful feedback. I may want to adjust my lifestyle according to the number it reads to get to the number I want, but that is all. It is no longer emotional. It is just a number that I use as a checkpoint.

May the placement of your Golden Sun above your head or the number on your acceptance gauge be a helpful checkpoint for you and not as a weapon of judgment.

Now, hold your bubble up and ask for a divine blessing. You are asking for a blessing from the Universe, God, Source, your highest self, Mother Gaia, your Orixás, the Greater Good, or whatever Higher Power you believe in. This step ensures that you are calling in this manifestation with grace and in the highest order for your specific path and purpose. The blessing can take whatever form best suits you. It may appear as light wrapping around your manifestation bubble, fairy dust sprinkled on your bubble, or it may feel like a warm hug from within. Trust however you receive this affirmation.

Case Study

Laura—From Grinding to Glowing

Laura was known as a manifesting queen long before she learned how to consciously manifest. She had a rags-to-riches story and was revered for being a self-made success. Then it happened—the manifestation of her dreams! Laura fell in love with someone who had all the qualities she had ever hoped for in a partner and more, including considerable wealth. You would think she would have been happy. Instead, Laura was confused. She had built her entire identity around working hard for her money and didn't know if she could be in a partnership that offered her the luxury of not working.

Energy works in mysterious ways. Having climbed her way to the top, Laura had embraced her reputation as a tenacious, disciplined, hard worker who never asked for handouts. She was so focused on her work that she was relatively unattached to the idea of manifesting a romantic partnership. Of course that's what she wanted, but she didn't feel like she *needed* it or was desperate for it. She was proudly independent.

Laura was in the final part of her manifestation process—giving abundant thanks—to accept and receive her dreams coming true. At the same time, she kept searching for flaws. She hired a private detective in an attempt to find out if her fiancé had any secret agendas for their marriage and she even wondered if he secretly trafficked humans. She was convinced her Prince Charming was too good to be true.

The investigator came up with nothing—Prince Charming was real! Because everything Laura had in her life was earned through blood, sweat, and tears, she couldn't believe that love could come so easily—not only that, but that her love could include financial security. All her dreams were coming true in magnitudes far greater than she ever imagined! So, what was the problem?

Laura had to learn to become as great at receiving as she was at giving. It made her feel vulnerable and uncomfortable, but being the hard worker she is, she rose to the challenge.

Laura learned to manifest ease and acceptance. Her challenge was not in creating the manifestation, but rather, letting the process be easy. Remember how manifestations are always a cocreation with the universe? Laura was prone to forgetting the "co" part and acknowledging that she creates in partnership with the universe. She had been relying on logic and forgot to make room for magick. So she began practicing her Manifestation tool with extra emphasis on the accepting and receiving part.

Receiving can be so humbling. Laura realized that before honing this tool, she was trusting more in her hard work than in her own powerful, radiant light. Through the power of the Manifestation tool, she learned how to trust in love, benevolence, and *ease*. She decided to go through with the wedding and continues to expand her ability to receive. Her manifestations continue to exceed her wildest dreams and provide her with opportunities for endless spiritual growth.

Completing the Manifestation

To complete this manifestation exercise, we recommend that you apply one of these three steps:

Release. You may watch the bubble float away into the universe never to be seen again. This practices trust and the art of allowing. This suggests that what is meant for you will not pass you by. Your trust in this concept will only accelerate your actualization process.

Embody. Visualize bringing the manifestation bubble in close to your heart, and watch it expand into every single cell in your body. This method declares that whatever you manifested is already yours and allows you to vibrate from that consciousness, and thereby accelerate its actualization process.

Plant. You can visualize planting the manifestation bubble and watering it daily to keep in integrity with the soul of this manifestation. Each time you water this manifestation plant, you remind yourself of your highest self. You remind yourself that you are worth it and that you deserve it. By honoring this intention over and over, you become familiar with it and gradually expand your consciousness to gently receive it in physical form.

You've come so far! How does it feel to be working this imagination muscle? You are nearly finished with the book, so by now you have done quite a bit of imagining! It's funny how children are asked to use their imagination all the time, but at some point we begin to imagine less and less. Even as teenagers involved in all kinds of creative activities, neither of us did much conscious imagining—at least not the way we are doing here. People often tell us that the visualizations they experience through these tools are like mild hallucinations or dreams.

Dreams and our imagination can be gateways to our intuition, which can lead to our self-acceptance and authenticity. When we get to this place, we are so much better equipped to walk through life with confidence, know where our energy ends and someone else's begins, and how to treat ourselves and humanity with openness, acceptance, and compassion.

USING THE MANIFESTATION TOOL

Take a moment to close your eyes and practice visualizing the steps of the Manifestation tool.

Step 1: Imagine in as much detail as possible the scene, tone, and environment where your manifestation actualizes.

Step 2: Focus on yourself accepting and receiving your manifestation as though it is happening in real time. Experience gratitude and bliss by acknowledging why this manifestation is meaningful to you.

Step 3: Finally, either release, embody, or plant your manifestation and trust the process.

Start Simple

As you begin using this tool, I recommend that you start by manifesting something that you are unattached to and then work up from there. An example of this working for me revolves around something quite simple: a pair of socks.

In 2010, I got into a confrontation with a man on a street corner in New York right after I finished teaching a manifestation class. He told an inappropriate joke that made my blood boil, so I schooled him on it. He apologized profusely. In seconds, we both went from shouting to laughing to talking. Amidst all the commotion, it did not even occur to me that he was positioned on that street corner to sell socks! I bought three pairs from him without even realizing that the example I had repeated over and over just moments earlier while teaching my class had to do with socks! I unintentionally manifested socks!

But I wasn't the only one with new socks. The following week, I shared this story with the class and half of them had unintentionally manifested new socks, too! One of them found a pair she had never noticed before in her home, another received socks as a random gift, someone else received a pair from her sister who was cleaning out her closet, and a different student bought a pair like I did without realizing it was the manifestation example from class. And none of us actually wanted new socks. But I must have mentioned that word enough times for our subconscious minds to get to work. I have been sharing that story ever since to illustrate just how easy it is to manifest when we don't have attachment to outcome.

Case Study

Tom—From Sad and Single to Super Spiral

Tom had wanted to fall in love for as long as he could remember. It was his number one goal. Naturally, when he learned this manifestation exercise, he used it to conjure up love. And love he conjured. Almost instantaneously! The romance moved fast, and before they knew it, he and his partner were living together and planning a future.

Tom's partner's job moved them from Los Angeles to New York City, but Tom was not excited about this move. Tom loved his hometown, family, and community. His career as an actor was finally taking off, and he didn't want to compromise his connections and throw away all the effort that he had invested in making it in the industry. He loved his life exactly as it was, but he was in love, and because he would do anything for love, he moved.

When they got to New York, much to Tom's surprise, his career expanded. He was cast in a Broadway show within months. He found a wonderful, supportive community in the industry and felt more at home than he could have ever imagined. Career growth following romantic growth is a classic example of a manifestation spiral. Tom also conjured up a new home, a new community, and a greater sense of purpose all through accepting and receiving his blessings while not worrying about how they came together.

Tom couldn't remember a time in his life when he felt this great. It felt like everything was going his way, which was a foreign feeling to him. He was having a hard time believing in his luck and enjoying his new elevated life.

The Manifestation tool works on the subconscious level of your mind and may sometimes surprise you. As Tom did the visualization, he was surprised to find himself in New York. He loved his life there! He valued his community, and it felt like everything was falling into place with greater grace in New York than he had experienced in Los Angeles. He saw himself exploring the city and all it had to offer with greater zest. The manifestation wasn't that different from his current reality.

When Tom got to the part of the visualization where it was time to bless his manifestation with gratitude, he had a realization: While focusing on manifesting love, Tom had also manifested *self-love and self-worth*. Tom had become a magnetic, manifesting force! Repeating the Manifestation tool regularly helped Tom ground into all of his dreams. He had an easier time accepting them in reality after getting familiar with them through visualization. He now utilizes this tool to help him transition into all new beginnings.

Your Manifestation Tool

You are here! The final lesson of this book! You manifested this! Think about it—you likely called in this book before you even knew it existed.

Were you desiring greater self-understanding? Maybe you have been searching for answers the internet isn't capable of providing you with? Perhaps you simply expressed curiosity or interest in metaphysics or maybe you are seasoned in energy work and were looking for a new take?

This book would not be in your hands if it wasn't a manifestation of yours. It was a manifestation of ours, too. Tim and I are so elated that our dreams and worlds have collided in this way!

You have been manifesting your whole life. With the help of your Manifestation tool, you are able to do so in a more meaningful, conscious, and empowering way. Now you can conjure objects, experiences, and sensations through visualization! How cool is that? You have the ability to manifest the life you desire. Just, wow! And the best part? You are learning how to trust in the process and remain unattached to the outcome. You trust that what is for you won't pass you by, and you live your life as though you know that. You would feel blessed by any one of your manifestations coming true, and you acknowledge that you are a blessing to these manifestations.

Just like the rest of the tools, your Manifestation tool serves as both a diagnostic and a healing modality. You will notice that your manifestations will change as you change. Your acceptance gauge offers you a sneak peek into your subconscious mind and how worthy you are feeling at any given moment. While you are visualizing, creating, and delighting in all you desire, you are calming your nervous system and flooding your body with beautiful, lovely endorphins. And you know what you are not doing? You are not stressing, worrying, procrastinating, or even thinking about your to-do list. This is my kind of energy medicine!

All of the energy tools you have learned through this book will help you better understand yourself, heal yourself, and command the energy in your life so that every day can be a fantastic day if you wish it to be. What sets the Manifestation tool apart from the others is that you are not only commanding the energy of your day, you are commanding the energy of your future. You are here on purpose. This tool helps you feel so and helps you live your life in a way that expresses your purpose.

What you manifest into your life is not as important as what you become. This tool can be one of your greatest allies in spiritual growth and self-realization.

Chapter Summary

The Manifestation tool is most useful in moments when you have identified an object, experience, or sensation that you would like to bring into your life. This is a wonderful, whimsical way to align with what is divine. Use your Manifestation tool when you want to actualize something that will improve your life or when you are ready to level up and align with your future self. In general, this tool is great for adding more value to your life.

A beautiful side effect of using the Manifestation tool is that you will also feel greater connection to and compassion for all.

Use your Manifestation tool with these three easy steps.

Step 1: Imagine in as much detail as possible the scene, tone, and environment where your manifestation actualizes.

Step 2: Focus in on yourself accepting and receiving your manifestation as though it is happening in real time. Experience gratitude and bliss by acknowledging why this manifestation is meaningful to you.

Step 3: Finally, either release, embody, or plant your manifestation and trust the process.

Tim and I agree that this tool is one to spend some time on. Linger in the manifestation for a little while. Just hang out as this version of you in this version of your life.

There are times when you won't have the luxury of time and will have to rush through the steps, like I did when skydiving. However, I was only able to rush through while skydiving because of the huge amount of time I had already devoted to this tool before I had that experience. I had been practicing it for years before that adventure. Just like any artist or musician knows, it takes hours and hours to perfect a skill, and it was these hours of experience that allowed me to execute the actualization I experienced in a matter of seconds. The time you invest in this tool now can hone your manifestation skills so that you are not at the mercy of time later. May all your dreams pleasurably manifest with ease, grace, and flow!

SELF-ASSESSMENT

Ask yourself the following questions. On a scale of 1 to 5:

_____   *How magnetic and deserving am I feeling right now?* (Where 1 is "More like unworthy and cursed. I never get what I want," and 5 is "I feel like the luckiest person alive sometimes! All my wishes are coming true!")

_____   *What is my relationship with desire?* (Where 1 is "Ugh. I hate it. It tortures me," and 5 is "I've embraced desire as a part of life and find it adds value to my life. Desire brings out the best in me.")

_____   *What would I do if all my dreams abruptly came true?* (Where 1 is "Gosh, that sounds a little intimidating and anxiety-provoking. I don't know what I would do," and 5 is "Eeeeeee! I would celebrate, naturally! I would integrate them all into my life with so much gratitude.")

_____ *Do I feel worthy of everything I want?* (Where 1 is "Nope. I feel inadequate and sometimes experience shame" and 5 is "Are you kidding me? I was born for this!")

AFTERWORD

It has been our absolute honor and pleasure to accompany you on this journey of intuitive development. You are a skilled intuitive, fully empowered with the tools to better understand yourself and to be your most authentic self. Now you know what to do when you feel unsteady, confused, or out of touch with yourself in any way.

As you practice these tools, you will continue to develop an intimate relationship with them and make them your own. You will recognize specific moments in which they prove incredibly useful that probably did not occur to you when you first started learning them. Along similar lines, you will also sense significant overlap with the tools and may find that, for example, a Separation tool works better for you than a Grounding Cord tool for a particular scenario. Go with whatever works best. Even after you master the tools, you will likely gravitate to some more than others and use them in different combinations at different moments in time. For this reason, we encourage you to crack open the book from time to time to rekindle your relationship with the different tools.

As you now know, these tools have changed our lives, and like Bostwick, who brought these tools to the Western world, we want to shout about them from the rooftops! It's likely that you, too, will have this experience. Most people who learn these tools tend to feel called to share them with friends, family, and strangers alike. That said, we have found that when we are really working these tools, people tend to notice a shift in us and will likely ask what has caused it. The most effective thing we can do for others is to teach them how to heal themselves. We can do this by sharing these tools with them as opposed to attempting to become their healer. When people are ready to learn, they will usually ask. If they are not asking, it is best to honor that.

What's next? From our vantage, your next step is crystal clear: Now is your moment to dwell in the full acceptance and unconditional love of all that you are, the deep know-ingness of your highest self, and the courage to be the most authentic version of yourself. It is time to listen to the call of your inner voice, to meet it with an open heart and a gentle mind, and to move forward on your path with greater clarity, confidence, and calm.

We love you and are eternally grateful for the opportunity to have connected with you and exchanged energy with you in this profound way.

From the fullness of our hearts,

Deganit and Tim

FAQS

Here are just a few of some commonly asked questions. We'd love to know yours! Message us at hello@nuurvana.com. We love growing with you!

What is the relationship between energy and information?

Almost everything imaginable, when broken down into its smallest particle, is energy: our bodies, our relationships, information we receive, and more. Even though information in its essence is neutral, because we are human, we attempt to make sense of it, which involves judgment and creates an energetic charge.

What is the difference between charged and pure/natural/ neutral energy?

Charged energy is what we often run off of in our daily lives. Charged energy is energy created by the collective consciousness. This type of energy comes about from the shared experience of being human. Feelings like fear, joy, and grief are all part of this realm of charged energy. We learn to experience these feelings. This kind of energy is human-made rather than pure energy.

When we are running off of charged energy, we are reacting to the ego rather than spirit. You could say that charged energy is energy that has been assigned value. Take for example, when kids fall down and cry: They are not usually reacting to the experience of pain, but rather to their parents' having assigned the experience of falling down with pain or disappointment. Kids cry because they see their parents fear their falling. When we are young, we learn that falling down is bad, that it is a mistake—all of this is charged energy surrounding an otherwise pretty neutral and natural growth experience.

Likewise, when we hear the word *pain*, we all tap into a collective idea of what pain is and we feel it without even hearing the rest of the story. We mentally go there so quickly because we have learned what pain is. Be honest, have you noticed any change in yourself after having read the word *pain* repeatedly? We barely have a chance to question it or respond to it with authenticity; thus, we're highly susceptible to experiencing the associations and biases of pain each time we read the word *pain*.

Can you explain a bit about what the colors going down the Grounding Cord tool represent?

All the colors we are letting go of represent charged energy: the "shoulds," the to-do lists, all the stuff we have learned to react to and have accumulated. In Daoism, it is said we are all born with a diamond in our center. This diamond is our essence, our intuition.

Yet, when life happens to us and we begin to take part in the charged energetic realm of being human, dust starts accumulating on the gemstone. This dust is not energy; rather, it is human interpretation. For example, let's say you get a B in a class and feel bad about it because a B is not an A, and you have come to believe that a B is less than perfect. This is a value being assigned, a human inter-pretation. That's a little dust settling on your stone.

As we move through life, all kinds of dust settle on our stone, and this dust doesn't only represent the negative; it also represents positive values. For example, overly identifying with the grade A as being perfect is another layer of dust. Either way, this dust is not the neutral, pure gemstone. These grades are not the essence of you. Instead, they represent a human value covering up our pure diamond essence. And so we begin to respond to the world from the dust rather than the gemstone. We start to see ourselves and our lives as a story made of dust rather than our essence. But if we wash off all the dust, we are all essence—intuitive, psychic, spirit, energy vortexes. Our essence is always there, it's just covered in dust/life/story.

It's kind of hard for many of us to distinguish our story from our essence because we have so long identified with our story. We think we are the dust. It's like the saying, "You're a human being, not a human doing." We are so used to defining ourselves by what we do rather than who we genuinely are. So the more we let go of the dust, the more we start connecting with that gemstone, and then we have that aha moment. Synchronicity starts to reveal itself. Life just starts getting more and more synchronistic. Things that don't normally happen easily start to happen faster and faster and easier and easier.

A big part of recognizing this essence is beginning to rec-ognize what is *not* that essence—all that other stuff, all those other thoughts. Recognizing the difference between energy and interpretation, or the human experience of the ego. See, the human experience is to want to make sense of everyone and everything, and therefore, the mind starts processing everything. And with each process, another layer of dust is likely to accumulate on your diamond.

When you're grounding out colors, it's the dust that you are releasing. It's like polishing your diamond.

Can you talk a little bit about the importance of learning these tools experientially instead of cognitively?

Yes, this course is experiential rather than cerebral. We begin to experience it in such a way that cannot be put into words. You begin to feel it. The one hangup people encounter in this work is trying too hard to comprehend energy. This often happens with people going through breakups. People always want to know why, but energy is just energy. People want everything to make perfect sense, but that usually only happens later—hindsight is 20/20, right?

Letting go of the colors and sending them down our grounding cords is letting go of interpretation and trying to make sense. It's interesting. Sometimes if we are searching too much for meaning, we are blocking ourselves from the light. The meaning we are seeking is usually bigger than the one thing we want it to mean. When we just accept things, the energy just flows through us.

Acceptance and judgment—where *judgment* means nothing more than trying to make sense—don't always work well together. When we are trying to assign a value to something, we are judging, trying to make meaning. By trying to assign value, we are not accepting it exactly as it is, and this process is not peace-producing. This is stepping out of our spirit and into being human.

I appreciate that the Center of Your Head tool values receiving information with neutrality, rather than with judgment, as humans normally do with information. At the end of the day, why not just try to reside at the center of your head and ignore the judgment-based human experience altogether?

It is important to understand the human experience because it allows us to relate to each other and connect with one another. We are an interdependent species and we thrive when in community and when feeling fulfilled with our connections. Relationships are spiritual contracts and they help us evolve. A harmonious balance of the spiritual and the human offers sustainable fulfillment.

We are born human for a reason. How we respond to the dust on our diamond (see the previous response) allows us more access or less access to the diamond. This perspective also resonates with the quote from *A Course in Miracles* that reads, "All encounters are holy encounters," which means that every interaction is fodder for learning. No matter whether it is good or bad, all experiences provide us with opportunities for growth.

It's wonderful to reside in the center of your head as a way of grounding spirit into your body or living in heaven on Earth. Living in isolation in the center of your head, however, and ignoring the judgment-based human experience altogether would leave you feeling quite lonely and disconnected. This is because humans need to belong and belonging happens in a world of meaning. Without meaning, there is no belonging. These tools are intended to be life skills to help you connect with the world around you rather than to dissociate from it.

When we are asked to see where the energy is in our space, what are we looking for? Is this something that we will just notice more as we practice these tools?

All this means is just noticing where your thoughts or mind go when that question is posed. When you actually close your eyes and scan your space, you will notice areas of greater and lesser density. You might observe a thick fog in your chest area and no energy in your feet. Or maybe all the fog is at your feet, but you don't notice any energy in your head. You may also notice different colors, textures, or sensations in different areas of your space. When energy is hanging out in a particular area, you are experiencing some sort of stagnation. If you are in good health, your energy is not just hanging out in one place; rather, it is flowing throughout your space. Flowing is harder to notice because it represents health. Our strengths are often harder to recognize whereas our weaknesses are consolidated energy, and when you are hung up on something, it gets noticed. Acknowledging it allows us to open up to other things, other ways of feeling.

What is clairvoyance and how does it relate to intuition?

We're all born intuitive. *Clairvoyance*, literally clear vision, is just one way of accessing your intuition. It's going to help you see beyond what meets the eye. It will help you clearly see whatever situation there is. There are plenty of ways to tap into your intuition; we have found this to be the most neutral path. Clairvoyance is just seeing things as they are without judgment, feelings, or opinions. Rather than seeing disaster as horrible, a more neutral perspective would just see it as information. Neutrality is clairvoyance. That is why we use the Center of Your Head tool to gain a neutral perspective.

✳—— ACKNOWLEDGMENTS ——✳

We are grateful to have been surrounded by so much love and support throughout the creation of *Imagine*. To our dear friends, family, and clients who championed us along the way—we are truly touched by your belief in us and this project. We would especially like to thank Nassrin, Avi, Eli, Seema, Daisy, Nancy, and Murph.

Our gratitude extends to Lewis S. Bostwick and the Berkeley Psychic Institute for sharing these ancient practices with the Western world. Thank you, Kayhan Ghodsi, for being the one to hand these tools down to us, and Andrew Carter, our Vibration Buddy, for nudging Deganit to teach these practices in the first place. Those early days in their shared Brooklyn home, filled with intimacy and curiosity, were the perfect fertile ground for the seeds of this book to take root.

To all the brilliant members of our Nuurvana community—the students of nu it who have been with us from the start, including our beloved Golden Girls, Krista, Jenny, and Dena; and the Guiding Lights, Crystal, Illi, and Melini, who have carried this lineage forward—our hearts overflow with appreciation for you.

To Diane Petrella and Ax Axford, your enthusiasm and encouragement kept us grounded and aligned throughout this process. To our generous lightworker friends—Jo-Ná Williams, Amina AlTai, and George Lizos—you were among the first to open doors for us to share these tools with a broader audience.

We would like to give a special thanks to Marilyn Allen— your warm encouragement, your belief in us and this project, and your gentle guidance from the start made all the difference. Emma Mildon, thank you for introducing us to Marilyn, sharing your wisdom, and cheering us on like only you can.

To our family at Hampton Roads and Red Wheel/Weiser— Michael Pye, Christine LeBlond, Eryn Eaton, Sylvia Hopkins, and Sarah Harker, as well as Rebecca Rider and Maureen Forys of Happenstance Type-O-Rama—we feel so seen and heard by you and are grateful for your collaboration.

Because Deganit is Iranian and her first spiritual teachers were Sufi poets, opening each chapter with a Sufi quote felt like a natural nod to her roots and this work's lineage. The epigraphs used are from *Hafiz's Little Book of Life* by Erfan Mojib and Gary Gach.

To Anita Moorjani, your advice, mentorship, and encouragement have been nothing short of transformational. Kari Schroeder, Bascom Guffin, and Suzanne Guillette, thank you for your sharp eyes, thoughtful edits, and compassionate coaching—you helped make the words sing. Amy Chan and Amy Mercree, your generosity in sharing your writing with us and offering endless support kept us inspired.

To Lance Morosini, for your expert eye and creative input; to Marika Frumes, for your devotion to spreading this work far and wide; to Serhii Skachko, for being the first to illustrate these tools so beautifully; and to Jillian Kornsweig, for crafting a digital home for them—thank you for being guardians of our vision.

To the brand partners who believed in us before the book had pages—*goop*, The Spa at the Four Seasons, Unplug Meditation, Alo Yoga, and the Institute for Integrative Nutrition.

And to the individuals who welcomed us into their worlds: Elise Loehnen, Gwyneth Paltrow, Jasmin Perez, Kiki Koroshetz, Tara Cruz, Suze Schwartz, Anna Glennon, and Jamia Wilson, thank you for seeing the light in this work and helping us share it.

Finally, to Bentley and Andre, our beloved friends turned spirit guides, you continue to teach us the boundless, unconditional love that pulses through every page of this book. To Louise Hay, our counsel, and to every being—seen and unseen—who whispered wisdom and trust into our journey, this book is a testament to your loving guidance.

ABOUT THE AUTHORS

Dr. Deganit Nuur, DACM, LAc (she/her), is a world-renowned spiritual teacher, celebrity clairvoyant intuitive, acupuncturist, columnist for *goop*, resident healer at The Four Seasons NYC and LA, author, and speaker. Founder of Nuurvana Clairvoyant Healing and named one of the "Top 15 Intuitives Worldwide" by *goop*, Deganit has been featured on the *Today Show* and *Good Morning America*, and has been written up in *The New York Times*, *Forbes*, *Vogue*, and *Vanity Fair*. Deganit has been practicing for nearly twenty years, has guided over twenty-three thousand sessions, and has taught the tools presented in this book to over five thousand students including activists and thought leaders worldwide. For more information check out nuurvana.com.

Tim Murphy, PhD (he/him), is a cultural anthropologist, teacher, writer, longtime friend, and student of coauthor Deganit Nuur. For the past twenty years, Tim has taught college courses and presented research on social inequality and belonging in the US and abroad. Tim is just as inquisitive, thorough, and methodical about his cultural explorations as he is passionate about empowering students and all those in his orbit. Tim helps readers of this book understand how intentionally employing these tools empowers them to change their own realities.

TO OUR READERS

HAMPTON ROADS PUBLISHING, an imprint of Red Wheel/ Weiser, publishes inspirational books from a variety of spiritual traditions and philosophical perspectives for "the evolving human spirit."

Our readers are our most important resource, and we appreciate your input, suggestions, and ideas about what you would like to see published.

Visit our website at *www.redwheelweiser.com*, where you can learn about our upcoming books and also find links to sign up for our newsletter and exclusive offers.

You can also contact us at *info@rwwbooks.com* or at

Red Wheel/Weiser, LLC
65 Parker Street, Suite 7
Newburyport, MA 01950